FOOTPRINTS OF HOPE

'A remarkable book, a remarkable journey, by someone who knows a remarkable God. I have personally known Kate and Peter for a number of years and it has been a great privilege to see the evident grace of God upon their lives. I recommend this book to inspire your journey through life.'

Anthony Henson, Newfrontiers, Lincoln

'Brilliant. This book will challenge you, encourage you, bless you because through it all we see a trust and reliance upon God which surpasses what many of us venture to have. Kate is an inspiration to all she meets and ministers to, she emanates the love of God, His power and strength.'

Gail Millar, Torch Holiday and Retreat Centre

'Thank you for the honour of reading your book. This was a privilege and an amazing story. I really felt that you have a message of hope. . . . Thank you for your courage and for sharing your story!'

Rachel Hickson, Heartcry Ministries

'The inside story of a life miraculously made whole by God and lived in the flow of His Spirit. Suffice to say, it is a great read – moving, challenging, inspiring.'

Dr Gordon Temple, Chief Executive, The Torch Trust

Mission Possible Ministries

Bringing the healing power of God's love
to His people

www.missionpossible.org.uk

Footprints of Hope

God Has Great Plans for Your Life
But What If . . . ?

A Powerful Story of Faith and Restoration

KATE MANCEY

To, Anthony & Gill,
with our love,
Kate & Peter
Rom 15:13

THANKFUL BOOKS

Copyright © Kate Mancey 2009

First published 2009

Published by Thankful Books
P.O. Box 2118, Seaford BN25 9AR.

ISBN: 978 1 905084 20 3

*Many of the names in this book have been changed for reasons of
confidentiality.*

Book design and production for the publisher by
Bookprint Creative Services, <www.bookprint.co.uk>.
Printed in Great Britain.

To Peter, my wonderful husband and greatest friend
and our two beautiful daughters, Rebecca and Victoria
who bring us so much joy.

May this book, prompted by the Lord Jesus, be a
permanent reminder of God's faithfulness, love and
leading throughout our life together and
His promises over us for the future.
To Him be the glory.

Contents

Acknowledgements

We would like to give a special thank you to:

Our parents David and Jean, Alfred (who we miss) and Margaret for all their love and support.

Bill and Eeva-Liisa, our lifelong friends who always make us smile.

Gavin and Pippa for their friendship, enthusiasm, love and encouragement.

The many special friends who have greatly blessed us and faithfully prayed for us over the years.

We pray our Lord Jesus Christ will bless and keep you always in His wonderful care.

Peter and Kate

Foreword

Every seven years a TV series appears on our screens, which is an experimental documentary following the stories of children born in the sixties through the traumas of childhood, into adulthood and their later years. As the camera records their progress we see how people develop, becoming what some might call 'nature and nurture' has shaped them to be. This book works in a similar way, allowing us an insight into what shapes a life of faith.

In her ruthlessly honest, emotionally engaging and vivid account we get to see, through Kate's eyes, the influences in a woman's life which make her into the person God intends her to be. We are never more truly ourselves until we allow God to shape us into His image. This is rarely an easy or pain-free process, but it does also open us up to the sheer exuberance and joy of experiencing God.

In the thirty years or so that Eeva-Liisa and I have known Kate and Peter and their daughters, Becki and Victoria, our friendship has grown and developed. We've always been able to laugh, cry and be completely honest and open with them. We have been witnesses to many of the things Kate faithfully writes about.

There are times when I have heard about miracles from people and wondered, 'Was it really like that? Is this person making a meal out of some fortunate coincidence?' It is easy to claim God to be speaking or blessing when it's nothing of the sort, just our wishful thinking. But this book is an account that is accurate and honest to the point of raw vulnerability. Kate and Peter have an integrity which we have seen over and over again.

As a Baptist minister, I've had the privilege and challenge of sharing part of their spiritual journey and also trying to unpack the meaning of the in-breaking actions of God, to the best of my theological ability. I find it sad that, too often, we don't ask too many questions of God or His Word; not because we trust implicitly, but because we just don't reflect enough on the everyday, the painful, awkward bits of our lives. For this is precisely where we find God, as well as the 'hallelujah' moments. This is the real world that Kate writes about.

In this book, you will be invited to confront issues of forgiveness, risk-taking, faith-stretching, honesty in prayer, justice and human dignity. The way Kate tells the story of her family's life and struggles quickly throws the spotlight on our own issues, reactions and prejudices. Like Eeva-Liisa and me, you may well find yourself asking, 'What do I feel about this? What kind of God do I believe in? How, then, should I live?' The one thought you won't be left with is, 'Well, that's easy for her to say.'

The Christian life is miraculous in its very nature. Jesus came not only to proclaim the Kingdom of God, but to bring it in His person and life and to call us to respond to it. That Kingdom is not some wonderful, golden age of miracles long ago when Jesus ministered in Palestine, nor just something that will happen one day in the far future, when Jesus returns. That Kingdom is active wherever ordinary, weak, sinful and vulnerable human beings *today* say 'Yes' to God's invitation to open their lives to His forgiveness, empowerment and guidance.

As Kate demonstrates, all this is not just for our individual, private blessing; it's for the benefit of our communities and indeed the whole world. There are no limits to the power, effect and extent of God's love. Kate and Peter's story is not finished. And neither is yours.

In this book, we are challenged to look again for the actions and love of God in the difficult times, the dark places, the humdrum parts of our lives. We are invited to trust God and move forward, not forgetting the pain, because that too has been part of our becoming who God wants us to be, but bringing all that has made up our journey so far to the God and Father of our Lord Jesus Christ who loves us and walks every step of the way with us.

So, as you read, laugh, weep and celebrate through this story, may God bring you joy in trusting His purposes for your life, as He has been doing for Kate and Peter.

Rev Bill Eugster

Jesus says, 'Follow me'

We can imagine Jesus striding forward, leaving His footprints for us to follow. His disciples, chosen individually by Him, following confidently behind, full of hope, full of vigour and ready for anything. Their excited chatter fills the air as they follow their Master wherever He leads them.

But what if your legs won't go that fast?

What if you can't keep up with the crowd?

What if you can't see where He's going?

What if . . . ?

What about me? If Jesus really is alive today, still choosing followers, would He really want a young, blind arthritic on His team?

ONE

Warning Signs

The day we moved house was a beautiful, sunny Easter-time day. The move itself went well and our two girls excitedly explored their new home with us. Discovering their rooms and placing favourite toys and books in new places, playing hide and seek behind the curtain in the bathroom, opening every cupboard door and drawer in the kitchen and, best of all, exploring the garden and making plans to turn the garden shed into their own den. It was an exhausting day but very satisfying as Peter and I sat over an evening cup of tea and talked about the future. Two tired little girls went happily to bed, shortly after to be followed by their equally tired parents. We got into bed, turned off the light and, as ever, within moments Peter was sound asleep. Then the nightmare began.

Nothing sinister, nothing scary, but a growing aware-ness of noise to ears already finely attuned to the slightest sound. Traffic noise; the constant low hum of engines, the crash of gear changes, the roar of acceleration at a nearby junction. I hid my head under the pillow, trying to rid myself of the din, but it remained.

Why had we not noticed this intrusion when we came to view the house? I remembered wandering round the garden, excited by its size and the mature shrubs and trees but the only sounds I recalled were the distant shouts of neighbouring children and the birds in the tree tops. The house had seemed perfect for our needs; more space inside and out, good location for schools and church, a bedroom each for the girls and even a separate dining room which could become a music room.

I breathed deeply, trying to relax myself and allow sleep to overtake me, but it was no good. The awareness of noise was impossible to escape. It seemed to be right inside my head, and no amount of sheep-counting or mental arithmetic puzzles could shift it. In fact, the volume of noise seemed to increase in my ears the more I tried to ignore it.

'Peter,' I whispered. But the steady breathing and stillness of his body beside me told me that he was deeply asleep.

Finally, after what seemed like hours, I got up and went downstairs. I stood in the living room hoping that an additional wall between the road and me would blot out the sound of traffic, but to no avail. The sounds in my head increased. I moved to the rear dining room but there was no comfort there either. I paced anxiously about the house until the early hours of the morning and then, desperate for sleep, went back to bed.

I could not bear this assault on my hearing. This particular sense was so susceptible, having to be my eyes as well as ears. I relied on it to tell me about people, objects, atmospheres and landscapes. In a world of physical darkness, my ears shed some audible light in my life. Now they were being battered and overwhelmed and were failing to filter out the unwanted. The familiar feeling of panic began to take hold again and I resolutely pushed it down. I could not go through that again. Instead, I tossed and turned anxiously until, just before dawn, I at last fell asleep.

'Wake up, sleepyhead! This is the first day in our new home, and you're sleeping through it!' It seemed only five minutes ago that I had managed to get to sleep, and now here were the encouraging tones of my husband, dragging me back to consciousness. I muttered at him and turned over, hoping for a longer doze. But he, who had slept like the proverbial log, was having none of it.

'Would you like a cup of tea, beautiful?' he enquired. 'And don't forget that we're going to your parents for lunch. We've got loads to do before then.' Somewhere in another part of the house, I could hear squeals and shouts coming from the children. It appeared that everyone was raring to go except me.

'I didn't sleep very well,' I ventured.

'It's always a bit difficult the first night in a strange place,' agreed Peter, cheerfully. It didn't seem to have affected *him*, I thought. I tried again.

'Does it seem a bit noisy here to you?'

'Noisy?' He sounded astonished. 'Not particularly, no. Well, not unless you count the girls!' It did sound as if they were up and about having a great time downstairs, so I guessed that they were enjoying a game together.

'I just noticed the traffic a bit in the night, that's all,' I said, trying to keep my voice controlled.

'Oh well, I expect we'll soon get used to things,' he said. 'I'll go and get that cup of tea; I'll check up on the girls at the same time.' He left the room, calling the girls as he went.

I curled up under the duvet, my heart sinking. I feared that my experience of the previous night was more than a reaction to a strange place, but I didn't know what to do about it. Peter obviously hadn't picked up on my distress, and I didn't want to spoil his enthusiasm about the new house by telling him. And besides, what could he do? We were here, and I would have to make the best of it.

The morning passed in a flurry of unpacking and sorting out. I installed myself in the kitchen, familiarising myself with the layout and carefully putting everything into cupboards and drawers, so that I would have a good chance of finding them again. Rebecca and Victoria treated the unpacking as an alternative Christmas, unwrapping items and shrieking in excitement as if they had never seen them before. More often than not, they then abandoned the item in favour of unwrapping another one. By lunchtime, we were glad to leave the multitude of boxes and go to my parents for a break.

Being back in the familiar environment of my parents' home felt comfortable. My earlier anxiety eased a little, and I relaxed as we sat down to eat. The girls chattered on, telling Granny and Grandpa about their new bedrooms and the various delights of their new home. Suddenly, as I sat listening to them, I was overwhelmed with sadness. Tears were running down my cheeks and I gasped as violent sobs began to wrack my body.

'Mummy! What's the matter?' both girls asked, their voices full of concern.

'It's all right,' Peter said soothingly, 'I think Mummy just needs a little rest.'

I stumbled up the stairs, clinging onto the banister rail and collapsed onto my parents' bed. Peter held my hand as I sobbed and sobbed. Bouts of deep emotional pain shook me; regrets for the very different life I might have had if only I'd been able to see, frustration at the many obstacles preventing fulfilment, fear for the future.

Attempts were made to persuade me to call out a doctor but I resisted vehemently.

'I can't bear any more doctors or hospitals. I've had more than enough of them.'

I started to cry again, panic gaining a hold as I gave way to the long-held fear of medical intervention. I begged Peter not to let anyone come and see me. I especially didn't want the girls to see me in such a state; I loved them so much and felt as if I had let everyone down, especially Peter and the girls. Peter assured me that he would not let anyone do anything I didn't want and after sitting with me for a bit longer, went down to see how the girls were getting on.

My dad came and sat by my bed. He talked to me in such a loving way as we had never done before and told me that I must just be myself and choose whatever I wanted.

I stayed in bed for three days. The girls thought I was just poorly and needed to sleep a lot. Peter must have been extremely anxious and, I know now, was praying fervently for God to intervene. I, on the other hand, could muster nothing; no thoughts, no prayer, no hopes for the future.

Once again, though, my strong will came to the fore and I roused myself, telling myself that I had a husband and children and that, however I felt, I had to go back and face it, and so I did. I say 'once again' because, several months previously, I'd had a similar experience, one which I had no desire to revisit but which forced its way back into my mind as I lay in the quietness on my parents' bed.

It was the previous Christmas and on the eve of the great day itself, I'd gone with my mum to the local supermarket, located in a large shopping centre, for a few last minute bits and pieces.

*   *   *

About half way around the shop I began to feel an overwhelming sense of panic. I felt so ill and for the first time thought I was going to pass out there and then. My heart began racing, I felt as if my chest would explode and a buzzing noise filled my ears, distorting the sounds around me of the supermarket announcements mingled with the Salvation Army band playing carols in the main thoroughfare. My grip on the trolley tightened and my feet became rooted to the spot. I was too frightened at first to express what was happening to me but knew I needed to do something. I reached out and touched my mum's arm; I shook it a little trying to convey the urgency of my need.

'Mum!' I seemed to choke out the word. 'Mum, I don't feel well. Please can we leave? I need some fresh air.'

She must have seen something in me that stopped the need for any questions as, within minutes, she had found an assistant and was asking for help. In my mind, I could only see the vast crowds of shoppers stretching as far as the eye could see and keeping me from my freedom. We were near the back of the supermarket and so thought that if only I could leave by the back exit it would be just a few more moments to hold on. By now, the rising panic within me had loosened my tongue.

'Is there a back exit for the staff?'

'Come this way,' replied the assistant, 'there's a rest room if you'd like to sit down for a while.'

All I knew was that I had to get out of the shopping area; the noise of the voices seemed to be increasing as if they were all pressing in on me and shouting in my ears. My mum took my arm and the assistant took the trolley, leading the way to the temporary sanctuary hidden behind double doors. She found me a chair and brought me a drink of cold water. My hand shook as I took it; somehow the drink to my lips brought me temporary comfort but how was I to get from here to my home? To my utter shock and disbelief, the assistant told us that there was no rear exit and the only way to leave was to go back through the main shop.

'Come on,' my mum said reassuringly, 'you'll be fine. You're just tired with all the preparations you've been doing.'

But this was more than just tiredness; I knew this was something I had never experienced before. I was gripped with fear, my mind rendered immobile to any other thought than the one sentence running through my head: 'You can't make it; you can't make it out of here'.

My mum took me by the arm and helped me up, placing my hand back on the trolley.

'Come on,' she said, 'its not far.'

I wanted to shout, 'Not far? *Not far?*'

The way ahead stretched before me, noise and darkness and a shopping trolley handle. That was all I had. I placed one foot in front of the other and looked steadfastly ahead. By now I was finding it hard to swallow. My throat was constricting more and more as I was jostled about in the crowd – impatient mums snapping at their children, crying babies also eager to leave, trolley wheels nipping at my heels. I remember thinking how strange it was, all these people and no one knows how I feel.

At last we left the supermarket only to be faced with the long walk through the shopping arcade to the car park. The route was so familiar, my sense of smell charting my path and encouraging me forward. Through the ever-increasing hubbub, the unmistakeable aroma of mince pies and freshly baked sausage rolls from the bakery mixed with the fragrance of fresh coffee from the café. On passed the smell of newsprint, herbs and spices, leather bags – I knew this pattern so well and eagerly awaited the waft of fresh fish. It usually made me wrinkle my nose but on this day it announced my escape and drew me like a magnet.

Of a sudden we were outside. The icy wind hit me, picking up my long black hair and wrapping it around my face. Impatiently I pushed it away and kept my grip on the trolley. At last, we reached the car. My mum opened the passenger door and I fell into its temporary safety. We didn't speak during the ten minute drive. I sensed her need to get me home quickly and I just sat there, almost holding my breath, rigid against what was going on inside me, clinging onto the only thought that had kept me going from the moment this 'feeling' had first hit me – 'home and Peter' – where I knew I would be safe. I held onto this thought until I reached home and climbed the three steps up to the front door and, in what felt like a daze, allowed Peter to take me into the bedroom and put me into bed. The relief and feeling of safety as I lay under the duvet was incredible. So long as I stayed here, in the peace and familiarity of our bedroom, I felt that everything would be all right.

I had suffered a massive panic attack, though I had not realised that this was the cause of my distress and would not do so for a long time to come. Of course, staying shut away in the bedroom would not be possible. I had a husband and two beautiful children to look after and, after all, I'd just become overly tired, hadn't I? It was the run up to Christmas, everyone felt like this . . .

TWO

Into the Darkness

Growing up in the nineteen fifties on the outskirts of Middlesbrough in the north-east of England was an idyllic life for me. The fast growing village of Marton was surrounded by corn-filled fields with hay bales to play on, cricket matches to puzzle over and low stone walls to hop, skip and jump along on summer days. The village post office had its own delights of white chocolate mice, parma violets and the aroma of stationery and string. The school, with its iron railings making a satisfying noise as we dragged our sticks along the side, and the wendy house where we spent many nursery hours entertaining our friends with tea and jam tarts made from dough. It must have seemed to all who observed that the little dark haired girl, so full of fun, with sparkling eyes and a smile, it was said, 'that would charm the ducks off a pond', would grow up to be a mature young woman, set for anything she chose; but life doesn't always work out the way we expect it to or even hope it will. However, a life released into God's hands will be all it was created to be. God had His hand on my life, as He has upon all of His creation.

By the age of seven it was discovered that I needed to wear glasses, as many children of my age did. I don't believe this was any great cause for concern at the time.

Katherine, aged six

I periodically visited the local eye infirmary, recalling inching my way down the pale green corridor and eventually entering the intimidatingly darkened consulting room at the far end. I hated the eye drops at first, as they made a most disgusting taste at the back of my throat, but after some months I began to administer them myself and hospital visits became part of my normal routine.

I enjoyed school life to the full locally at Captain Cook Junior School. I did sit near to the front in order to see the blackboard but this had its advantages, most especially at morning playtime, when I was one of the first in the daily playtime queue for a small bottle of milk with a straw. Our class teacher was Miss Russ, the headmistress, a formidable lady for her diminutive size, who would admonish us in her booming voice, 'And mind you drink it all to the bottom'.

I shared a July birthday with my best friend, Ann, celebrating with a party in the garden, playing musical statues and bumps, pass the parcel and pin the tail on the donkey. Birthday teas consisted of sausages on sticks, sandwiches, the great treat of plain crisps and lemonade, and to finish, frilly waxed-paper bowls full of orange jelly.

By the age of thirteen, I was settled in senior school with new friends as well as the old. I spent many happy days out and about on my pale blue Raleigh bicycle, heading out into the nearby countryside, rucksack strapped to my back filled with sandwiches, crisps and a bottle of fizzy pop to share with my then best friend, Jane.

However, I was soon to develop 'fat knees' and from a fashion point of view, for a girl in her teens, the arrival of the midi skirt was a great delight to me, replacing the need to wear the mini.

After many visits to our local doctor and an airy dismissal from him, 'It's just a case of housemaid's knee, nothing to worry about, probably just a teenage thing that will correct itself', my mum's insistence for further action to be taken resulted in an appointment being made for me to see an orthopaedic consultant.

This led to a further appointment with a rheumatoid arthritis specialist, who verified that this disease was indeed affecting my knee joints.

My mum must have had a private discussion with the specialist as, lying in my bed one night, I was suddenly aware that she was crying downstairs. I crept out of my room onto the landing and stood in the dark, shivering with both the cold and a mounting fear, as I strained my ears to hear the cause of the upset.

'It's so awful, David.' I heard my mum's voice between tears. 'She could be in a wheelchair by the time she's in her thirties.'

A wheelchair! I took in the horror of this totally unexpected information. A wheelchair – me in a wheelchair!

I pushed this information away as I crept back to bed. Crawling back under the covers, my feet searching for the hot water bottle, I reached for my blue rabbit hidden under the pillow. The desire for childhood security even at the age of thirteen needed to be met. As I curled up under the blankets I wondered what all this would mean. I had many questions buzzing around my mind but I knew I couldn't ask them. I wasn't supposed to have heard and so, as I eventually drifted off to sleep, I buried my fears for another day.

The solution for the podgy knees with floating kneecaps and a weakness in the joints was to have surgery, removing the cartilage and lining of the knee. These operations were carried out, one knee at a time, each knee requiring a month-long hospital stay and many months of daily visits for physiotherapy, which consisted of ice packs around the joint to reduce the swelling, electric shocks to build up the weak muscles and pool therapy to encourage flexibility in my joints.

Sitting in the garden at home, aged thirteen

My life at this time revolved around the hospital; it was a sometimes frightening experience as doctors arrived, poked and prodded, scribbled their notes and then left without a word of explanation. There were some happy times shared with physios and other children on the wards. We had visits from the hospital teachers who encouraged us in artwork, and the pale green hospital walls of our six-bedded room were soon covered in my artistic endeavours, usually portraying Dougal and friends from *The Magic Roundabout*. The highlight for us all was receiving Blue Peter badges for our cartoon drawings of Top Cat.

Whilst in hospital, I think concern for my eyes must have been growing as I recall being visited there by my eye consultant, but nothing was ever said to me to cause me to worry. I was, of course, away from normal school life by now and, indeed, far too weary to cope with such a daily routine as the arthritis caused me to sleep much of the time.

However, the return to school life came around eighteen months later. My senior school made arrangements for me to have all my lessons on the ground floor as climbing stairs was impossible and all science labs were on the upper floor. I was despatched to the sanatorium to do appropriate work. I felt rather isolated at these times but my friends would make up for this during free time. I didn't miss not being able to be involved in sport as I had always been fairly hopeless at such pursuits as athletics and netball, though I really loved playing right-wing in hockey and tennis in the summer months.

A great sadness was the loss of ballet. From being small I had loved dancing and was just about to move onto points, a special moment for any ballet dancer. I had thought that these operations would result in my being able to dance again but as the months wore on I began to realise that this was never going to happen. I would never be able to dance again, or run or enjoy my favourite sports.

I had loved going away youth hostelling with my dad; we would go away for a few weeks at a time during the school holidays and walk the North Yorkshire moors and coastline, trekking up steep hills, slithering down the other side in the pouring rain, laughing together as we skidded into each other at the bottom. Counting the one hundred and ninety nine worn steps up to Whitby Abbey where right at the top a hostel was situated. We would collapse at the top, breathless and starving. All these enjoyed moments too were to become only memories to live off and for the first time in my life I began to learn how to cope with disappointment as best I knew how, burying hope away to avoid future disappointment and wearing a brave face, the outward happiness required to make others feel comfortable.

During one of the study visits to the sanatorium, poring over a chemistry textbook I noticed the words on the page were beginning to blur. I don't recall any panic, I just looked at the words with interest and for no apparent reason I gently pushed against the edge of my eye and found that it seemed to refocus everything, so that became my solution for some weeks to come.

It was decided that I would change schools at this time. I had missed large chunks of education and a new start, a fresh approach to my catching up found me at age fifteen joining the fifth form of a girls' school. Margaret and Poppy soon became good friends and by now I was able to use the stairs, which meant I could be with my class throughout the day. This new beginning in my life was to be short lived, however, as my sight began to deteriorate once more and the manual refocusing technique I had adopted no longer had any effect. I didn't know what to do and so in true fifteen year old style, like an ostrich, I buried my head in the sand and hoped it would all go away.

I travelled to school each day on the school bus. One winter's morning as we gathered at the bottom of the hill in the crisp sunshine, I looked up to see if the bus was coming. The sun was in my eyes and I thought it was this that was distorting my view. However, as I continued to look I realised that I couldn't see anything but a blur in front of me. I began to panic inside, I could feel my face blushing as I looked around nearby me trying to make out the familiar uniform colours of dark brown and blue.

Straining my ears to pick up on familiar voices, I edged nearer and as they called out, 'Here's the bus', grabbing up their rucksacks and running towards the road's edge as they did so, I knew I just had to stick close to them. So, like a sheep in the centre of the flock, I placed myself in the middle of the group and was carried, as it were, onto the bus. My heart was racing; I didn't know what to do or say and so just grabbed hold of a seat edge and sat down. I chatted normally to my friends and they didn't seem to be aware that anything was any different.

Once again the charade began and on arrival at the school I started what came to be weeks of shadowing everyone, never daring to lose their nearness for a moment as we moved from classroom to classroom throughout the day; waiting for someone to go to the toilets so that I might go too and dreading being pounced upon by a teacher to read aloud. I stopped having lunch in the dining room, making excuses each day, as I thought someone would surely notice I was struggling to use my knife and fork, as the food on my plate became indistinct.

It was all exhausting but I didn't feel I had any other option; I was too frightened of what might happen to me if I told anyone and the fear of being found out drove me on. At home, which of course I knew so well, I used what sight I had to manoeuvre around the house with seeming ease, which helped to cover up my inabilities whilst using enthusiastic chatter as a decoy.

However, it all came to a crashing end when I returned to my old school to see a friend, Christine. I was waiting for her with a few other girls when in she walked.

'Hi Katherine,' she greeted me. She stood across the room in the doorway. 'How do you like my cords – great colour?'

'Yes,' I tentatively replied. She was only a blur in the corner.

'What about the top?' she went on.

'Fab,' I faltered. I felt flustered and tried to change the subject but she had realised something was wrong. As our time that afternoon went on, I knew she was testing me out but neither of us spoke out what we were thinking.

A few days later my mum received a letter from Christine telling her about my visit and her concerns about my eyesight. I came to realise later that she had done this out of love, as a friend, but at the time I felt so betrayed by her, upset and angry inside – was there no one that you could really trust?

On receipt of the letter, I was whisked off to my eye consultant where, in his darkened room, a deliberately placed chair became the downfall of my master plan and the truth was out in the open. He was very kind and gentle with me as I sat there, fighting back the tears as fear welled up within me whilst he explained that I would need operations on my eyes. Not more hospitals! My mind raced ahead and memories of the past came flooding back – hospital trolleys rattling their way down long corridors whilst I shivered with fear under thick white blankets; the smell of the operating theatre; injections, pain and feeling so alone.

The removal of cataracts was the solution, first the right eye, to be followed some months later by the left. This again was a frightening time for me with no way of escape; though the nurses were very kind I had no idea what was to be the outcome and the week's recovery after the first operation was spent flat on my back with my head fixed firmly between two sandbags, so as to stop me moving at all. Disgusting soup (usually vegetable) was fed to me through a feeder cup. The bits got stuck in the spout whilst the weak, flavoured water dribbled through.

This operation was not set to be a success. As a fairly new technique in those days for this eye infirmary, the eye had not been stitched down and I had apparently opened it whilst coming round from the anaesthetic and scratched it on the dressing, losing the sight in my right eye completely. This total loss of sight must have been discovered during the removal of the dressing. I recall the surgeon peeling it back; there was a nurse assisting him in the room and my mum standing by the bed. No one spoke as he shone a light into it.

'Try and keep it open as long as you can, Katherine.'

I tried hard despite the fact my eye felt so weak and kept watering. I was expecting to see perfectly, no one had told me otherwise.

'What can you see?' he queried. 'Can you see the light?'

There was nothing.

'It's just dark,' I said.

He replaced the dressing and patted my knee.

'That's all right, we'll see you tomorrow.'

I imagine conversations went on between the surgeon and my parents, but no information came my way. At that age I just accepted that all would be well and continued listening to my books and music tapes between visitors. A few days later I was sent home, still putting in eye drops and now waiting for a second operation to my left eye. I wondered what was happening about my right eye and why I couldn't yet see, but it was far too daunting ever to ask. I trusted them, after all, they had told me I would see and so it must be true.

The second operation took place and my other eyelid was of course stitched down this time. To my delight, one week later when the dressings were removed, I could see bright white worm-like things waving in front of my eyes as the surgeon once again asked if I could see anything. They were his fingers but everything looked so white and bright, it was startling. I returned home on 14th November 1973, the day of Princess Anne's wedding, and sat on the floor in front of the television with my special cataract glasses, taking short glances at her beautiful dress lifting in the breeze as she entered Westminster Abbey. It was an exciting day for me, and I totally expected to be seeing perfectly very soon.

At fifteen, though partially sighted, I looked forward to reading printed books again. I had always enjoyed this pastime and would look forward to Christmas and birthdays when a WH Smith book voucher for £2 would turn into a huge bag full of two-shilling paperbacks. Comics and magazines, too, were a great way of just relaxing in the garden sunshine or on my bed, losing myself in adventure or romantic stories. Cassette books just didn't have the same appeal and the memory of holding a book and smelling the new pages would fill me with longing and hope.

I missed my piano playing, too, and longed to be able to select some music and produce something satisfying through my fingers. I also looked forward to being able to go out on my own when I chose to and not having to always wait for someone else's free time; meeting up with friends and going shopping, choosing my own clothes. My mum was great, bringing clothes home for me but I often wondered what other girls my age were wearing – did I look like them, did I fit in? I didn't know and was too shy to ask, after all, she was so kind and I didn't want to seem either ungrateful or foolish to ask such things.

Over the next few months, the newly gained sight in my left eye slowly began to deteriorate until I had no sight at all, only darkness. I finally came to realise that I was now destined to be 'blind'. I hated that word – I was Kate, not blind. I couldn't say it and would use any other way of describing my sight loss to others; I couldn't even use that word 'blind' about others, either. It was as if saying it would make it a reality in my life and I didn't want it to be so.

As a resilient teenager and with the encouragement from my family and friends, however, I slowly began to accept this situation and learned to adjust to the necessary changes in my life. I was at home during the day as my parents were at work and so began to learn how to cook for myself. Just opening tins and buttering bread took a long time. We would line up tins in groups in the kitchen cupboard: savoury foods, fruit, cream, and then jars. I would shake the savoury tins at lunchtime, trying to identify the sound between beans and soup. I had very few disappointments on opening them and not too many culinary disasters. Baking, of course, was entirely different; learning to feel when a cake was ready and using my sense of smell to forewarn me of disaster became a part of kitchen life.

Learning which different textures of my clothes matched which colours and identifying pairs of shoes by certain patterns under my fingers; learning to feel the size of coins and different notes in my purse so that I didn't get flustered in shops with an impatient queue behind me; picking up other ways of recognising those around me by the way they breathed, their footsteps, the way they sniffed or coughed, were all ways in which I trained my other senses to become far more acute, compensating for my lack of sight. I still held the thought that this was only a temporary situation, as no one talked about it at home and the consultant didn't discuss my case in front of me. Not realising the full facts about my future, the false hope of someday seeing again kept me going. The real truth was that there was no cure, no further operations to restore my sight, no treatment of any kind; the damage was irreparable.

By now, my friends had dwindled to two faithfuls, Denise and Carol; the others, I think, didn't quite know how to approach anyone with a disability and were too embarrassed to cope with it all. As a result of this, I became quite self sufficient, out of necessity learning how to enjoy my own company and my music. I made hesitant steps towards learning the guitar (continuing with the piano at that time seemed impossible) and so I spent many hours learning to harmonise with songs playing on the radio. In particular, the Osmonds, The Beach Boys and

The Carpenters, with their close harmonies, captured my imagination and inspired me to take simple songs and begin to arrange them in three parts, a skill which God was, unbeknown to me, to use in my future.

Like any other normal teenager, I had boys on my mind too, but the idea of anyone being attracted to me now I was blind seemed impossible. As a young woman I felt very unattractive; though able to hide my still podgy knees with their scars, my face was another matter. I knew by touch that my right eye must look different to the left one and just wanted to hide my face away. The picture in my mind of myself was, of course, far exaggerated from the truth but it didn't matter how many times people told me I was 'pretty', I couldn't believe it. They were bound to say that weren't they? I used to stand in front of the mirror in the bathroom with the door locked and peer hopelessly into it – if only I could see what I looked like, I just couldn't remember at all.

In fact, there were times when small children would ask whilst almost sticking their little fingers in my eye, 'Why aren't your eyes both the same?'

Although I knew they were only small and knew no better, their remarks cut right through me and made me feel even more ugly; children always tell it as it really is. Of course, their parents were horrified and for their sakes I learned to put on the cheery smile.

'Don't worry, they're only interested,' I'd say reassuringly as I tried to distract them with a toy.

I parted my hair down the side so that my fringe would cover up most of my right eye but I longed to be elegant and beautiful like all the other girls my age, experimenting with hair styles, make-up and wearing heels, something else denied me because of my arthritis. I would sit and remember passing groups of older girls when on my way home from junior school. I would listen to them chatting away and looking so grown up, so sophisticated; I'd hoped that one day I might be like them but I knew now that could never be the case. I was destined to be clumsy, always on the arm of someone and most definitely alone in this dark place. So I spent many hours at night lying on my bed in the dark, listening to the dulcet tones of Donny Osmond and David Cassidy and dreaming of what might have been!

Having lost so much time in education it was decided that I would be taught at home by a number of different home tutors, as the only solution the education authority had at that time was to send me away to school. My parents wouldn't hear of it as I had too many other physical difficulties as well as my blindness. I'm so grateful to them for not sending me away, as I loved my home and didn't want to leave it. My home tutors all expected their subject to be attended to as a priority and my workload was great. With the use of my trusty tape recorder and a board to write on with elasticated lines strung across it to keep my writing straight, I took five O levels in one year and to my relief and utter amazement, passed them all.

Without knowing it, I was about to step into a new world, out of the safe environment of home where I was just 'Katherine', no labels, into a world who would view my disability as a problem to be overcome. But what was God's plan for my life, did He actually have one and if so, how would He bring it about?

THREE

New Beginnings

My one desire was to be a junior school teacher as both my parents were teachers and I had spent much time in my early years after school hours with them enjoying orchestra rehearsals, pantomimes and great artistic works, including a full size elephant and an igloo, built using papier-mâché in the corner of the classroom, a speciality of my father. During the years surrounding my physiotherapy treatment, I spent every afternoon in my mum's school, training a junior choir, recorder groups and teaching guitar. I helped various teachers in the classroom, too, listening to readers, story writing and generally helping out. Even when I lost my sight they continued to invite me into their classrooms, which was an enormous boost to my self esteem.

There were a number of teachers in their twenties and one of them, Miss Weightman, married during the summer and she asked me to be a bridesmaid. This was such a wonderful surprise to me to find that someone wouldn't mind having a blind bridesmaid at their most important day. Wearing my beautiful long dress and flowery hat, I felt pretty for the first time since losing my sight. I think I must have learned much from these enthusiastic young teachers and my great desire to teach was increased even further.

Nothing but teaching appealed, despite all attempts to dissuade me from this.

I applied for teacher training college and was asked to go for interview. It was very daunting as I sat there with a group of tutors and the principal firing questions at me.

'How will you cope with marking?'

'How would you know if a child was about to do something dangerous with a pair of scissors?'

'How will you deal with parents who don't want a blind teacher for their child?'

Apparently my answers must have satisfied them, as a week later, with great excitement, I received a letter offering me a place.

My mobility, or should I say lack of it, was my first and greatest hurdle at this time. As a little girl, I had seen pictures of blind people with white canes and the thought horrified me. It seemed so unladylike to me, perhaps because all the pictures I had ever seen were of old men, and so my thoughts turned to a guide-dog. We had a small Cairn terrier when I was young but that was my only knowledge of dogs; guide-dogs were little known or seen, it seemed, in our part of the country. We contacted the central office and after an assessment of my situation over the telephone it was decided that I would firstly need some kind of mobility training, as I had spent the past four years on someone's arm whenever out and about. The timing of all this training would be tight, as both my mobility and guide-dog training needed to take place before I began college in September 1976. I therefore left for a mobility training centre in Nottingham called Clifton Spinney. I had six weeks to become independent, not only with a white cane but in the home too.

This was my first encounter with blind people, approximately fifty of us, ages ranging from late teens into retirement. My time there was divided between unsuccessful attempts to teach me how to read Braille, more successful attempts to teach me how to stuff a chicken or iron a shirt, frustrating hours spent making cane baskets and frightening times out and about the busy streets with a white cane.

The white cane training was, of course, the main reason for my stay and this daily training was the source of my greatest fear each day. The moving of this cane from left to right, with the motion something mirroring a windscreen wiper, was meant to help me avoid all hazards on the way ahead. However, this never stopped wet overhanging tree branches from various gardens slapping me in the face – always an unexpected shock to the system. On another occasion, whilst heading down a pedestrian-only shopping precinct, unbeknown to me, a large delivery truck was parked and I gaily swept my cane exactly between the wheels at the rear of the vehicle and walked slap bang into the back of it! I think it was probably at this point that the idea of having a guide-dog grew on me to a far greater degree. Humiliation and pain were not two of the most desired things in my life!

It was there, at the age of nineteen, that I first encountered the general public and their sometimes unbelievably thoughtless and hurtful comments, made often in stage whispers, about my disability and appearance as a 'poor thing'. It was there that I began to create around me a shell of protection to cope with my lack of sight, putting on a mask for others and learning to laugh at myself before others could laugh at me. I became much more independent during my stay and the final week spent in 'the training flat' with just one other girl, Ann, being solely responsible for our own housekeeping, shopping, cooking, cleaning and entertaining guests each day, taught us skills that were to prove invaluable for the future. I've never made a cane basket since then, but I am the proud owner of a wooden plant trough, made during two rebellious weeks when my flatmate and I refused to do any more basketry and were seconded to the men's woodwork classes, where we wreaked havoc, drilling through the woodwork table in our enthusiasm!

It was at the Spinney that some sixth-form students came at weekends to talk with us and share the Gospel. For the first time I heard that Jesus Christ had died for me because He loved me, that if I had been the only person in the world He still would have died for me, He was crucified and buried but rose again on the third day so that I might know Him and receive eternal life and live in all His blessings. It seemed that this Jesus was real to them but I only sat quietly and listened. Memories of the Methodist Sunday school I attended as a little girl flashed into my mind: dressed in our Sunday best, we gathered in the schoolroom, perched on our little wooden chairs, clutching our pennies for the collection as we sang 'Hear the Pennies Dropping'. I loved these times – Sunday school trips onto the Yorkshire moors, games in the field, picnics and exciting Christmas parties.

As the years went by, however, and my sight deteriorated, I hid away in the church crèche, not knowing how to relate to my friends as I seemed to embarrass them. Even though it was a huge congregation, I was the only one there with any kind of disability. None of us seemed to know how to cope with it and the kindly ladies who looked after the babies seemed my safest option. Church became a boring place when required to sit in the adult service; it was something to be endured on a Sunday, just something you did, but I'd never questioned what we were doing there until now.

Having successfully completed, if not without some fears, my mobility training in Nottingham (a necessity before being accepted onto a guide-dog training course), I left for Forfar in Scotland to spend a month with a group

Out and about with guide dog, Solo

of twelve people and their new dogs, some first timers like myself, the baby of the group, and one gentleman in his seventies on his fifth dog! It was my first time to get about independently for many years and as I took my first scary steps on my own, clutching the handle of the harness on my beautiful labrador, Solo, I was off – trying to remember the routes told to me by the trainers and putting my confidence in my dog as we battled, on one occasion, through crowds of Rangers supporters who had stopped off enroute to their Saturday match. I began to realise I could put my trust in this dog wherever we were to go. I began to learn to relax whilst out and about with the public, finding that the dog took all the attention off me and was the easy route to get to know people.

We had some great times together as a group, including joint disasters to console each other in. A number of us, ignoring the skill of our dogs when walking a familiar route, coaxed them through some wet tar, which had to be laboriously cut out from in between the pads of the dogs feet. Not a popular time for us with the kennel maids. There was great hilarity and leg pulling from the trainers on occasions when, retrieving our dogs from the run, we would take the wrong one and spend the evening puzzling over why it would not respond to us as it always had. We spent an evening in the local pub playing darts, much to the shock of the locals, but very liberating for us. Then, for everyone, there was the dubious pleasure of eating haggis and chips on the way home in the minibus!

This time, coupled with college life in general and the making of a really good lifelong friend, Sheila, helped me to become a much more confident person. The freedom of not seeing reactions on faces somehow helped me to gain boldness in communicating to groups of people, a skill I did not realise at the time was part of God's preparation for the future.

I began my three year teacher training and was fortunate to be assigned to a tutor who believed I could succeed – though there were many who openly told me it was impossible. Senior pupils, perhaps, but a class of thirty or more small children? I had a team of readers for my set books and once again, armed with my tape recorder, took notes in lectures. Life in college was busy; I had learned to touch-type, a necessary skill to enable me to copy up recorded lecture notes and produce assignments. The compulsory foundation courses caused some interesting problems of their own: art and science in particular; but they enabled me to take time to think about how I would be able to teach these subjects to children. There was much fun between the hundred students in our year and although I was the only disabled student in the whole college I felt totally accepted and part of the furniture, just the way I liked it.

We had a lot of fun with my visual impairment. A darts match set up between myself and a male student, Dave, to raise funds for the Students Union, caused much amusement across the whole college. We raised a vast sum of money as almost everyone sponsored in my favour as they expected me to lose mightily. However, to his great shame and embarrassment, I beat him, four games out of six. We sometimes had visiting students from the local polytechnic, trying to enrol us for outdoor activities. My friends watched in great amusement as one young man talked me into, or so he thought, signing up for hang-gliding one weekend. His face was a treat as I thanked him at the end of our break time and extracted my dog from under the table. 'See you on Saturday,' I smiled and left him looking after me somewhat shocked and rather bemused.

During my second year at college, whilst browsing in the resources centre, I heard a voice for the first time. 'Mm, that's a lovely accent, wonder where he's from?' I mused.

'Are you looking for anything in particular?' the voice asked in my left ear. It was him.

'Just trying to look for some inspiration for my music course,' I replied.

'I'm Peter and I've a lot of folk music if you're interested?'

'Folk music,' I thought. I didn't know anything about that but the voice was lovely.

'Thanks.' I didn't know what else to say.

'Perhaps we could meet up one lunch time; I play the guitar, what about you?'

'Oh I'm a music student, so a bit of piano, recorder and some classical guitar.'

The next lunch time we met up in one of the practice rooms in the music department. Sure enough, he had brought his guitar and by now I knew his name was Peter and that, though originally from Essex, he had moved to Devon with friends some years ago and adopted a gorgeous Devonshire accent. He told me he was a Christian and I said I was too. He seemed very gentle and had a love for singing folk songs and, though self taught, played guitar amazingly. Our lunch time meetings became a daily event and he suggested the possibility of my going to Devon, perhaps in the summer.

I was shocked, not at the suggestion but at the thought of travelling somewhere far away on my own. My home town area was one thing but rail, coach or any kind of travelling alone? I realised for the first time that things were changing. There were new challenges arising in my life, but could I cope with them? Many fears filled my mind and though I sat looking at him, smiling and looking relaxed, my mind was running riot and my insides churning.

'What if I get lost? What about all the new people I'll need to meet? What if they're shocked by him having a blind girl with him? What if I make a fool of myself?'

Again, the desire to be elegant, beautiful, assured, rose up inside me. Every other female my age was all of these things, I could see them in my mind's eye, but there I was – flat shoes, fat knees, odd eyes and an ability at any given time to trip up, knock over and bump into anything that might be in my path.

'How can I do this?' I asked of no one in particular. 'There must be someone or something that can help me.'

The night of the college Christmas dance loomed near and I went into town with my friend, Sheila, another music student. We had become such good friends and spent much of our free time together. My parents had generously bought me a second-hand car which I named Whinnie, as its registration plate was WHN! This gave me more independence as I could offer the car as a means of a thank you

to those who would drive me about. Sheila and I set off to
town in pursuit of dresses for the event. I found one. My
mode of shopping was to move along the racks feeling
the material at a fairly rapid speed until I came across
something which felt good to my touch. I would then find
out what colour it was, and, if I felt that it would suit me
would ask for the appropriate size. On this occasion my
hand fell upon a beautiful soft material. I ran my hands
down the dress.

'It's full length,' I thought. 'Very floaty.'

'What's this?' My hands shaped a curved neck line and
at the base was what felt like a flower.

'It's a rose,' Sheila said.

'Not too sure about that,' I scowled. I didn't like anything that would draw attention to me, wanting to just
merge into the background.

'It's really pretty and very small, you're only a size ten,
after all,' laughed Sheila. 'Try it on.'

So I did. It slid over my head and fell softly down. I ran
my fingers over it. First the shoulders with the floaty cap
sleeves, then around the neck line and the rose and then
down my waistline and onto the hem. It certainly felt
good.

'What do you think?' I asked, sliding back the curtain.

'You look lovely,' Sheila encouraged.

'Really, are you sure? This rose thing doesn't look daft,
does it?'

'Not at all; get it, you look great.'

I removed my jacket very self consciously that evening
but the girls only gave exclamations of pleasure to each
other. All I could hope was that I didn't look out of place.
That was what was so hard. You just never knew. People
could tell you anything and would be too kind to say how
awful you looked. So with all my courage I set off to the
dance floor and there was Peter. I always knew when he

was coming towards me. My guide-dog's tail would wag
vigorously and she would accelerate forward.

'Hello,' I said, shyly.

'You look lovely.'

'Thank you.'

That evening we danced together most of the time.
Peter held me close and I felt very safe in his arms. He was
special, I knew it.

As time went on, we talked and talked. Peter was a 'born-
again' Christian. He talked to me often about his love for
Jesus and I began to realise once again that just 'knowing
about' Jesus wasn't enough; it was this personal relationship that people had, a relationship that transformed their
lives and gave them purpose, peace and great joy. Having
come to know Jesus only six months before coming to
teacher training college, Peter had made two decisions.
The first was to get involved in a local church and the
second was to have nothing at all to do with women! It
seemed like God had different plans for him.

During the months of getting to know each other I
came to realise that, although I had been brought up in
a Christian home and knew some of the Bible and even
prayed sometimes, I had to make a decision myself, to ask
Jesus Christ into my life. Peter took me along to his church,
a lively Baptist church in Redcar, a seaside town where he
rented a room in a nearby house.

To be honest, I was so shocked – everyone was really
happy and relaxed and had a level of joy I had never seen
in church before. What struck me most of all was that this
'life in Jesus' was not just lived out at church, but on visiting many of their homes and families it was apparent that
this was their whole life.

I sat through many sermons, which told me that a truly
fulfilled life was only found with Jesus; and I believed it.
But no one actually told us what to do about it. It was for

me to ask Jesus into my life, to receive His forgiveness for all that I had previously got wrong, to invite Him to be Lord of my life and fulfil His plans and purposes through me. His plans would be the very best for me. I didn't share my situation with Peter as I loved him so much and was frightened I might lose him; after all, he thought I was already a Christian. I'd thought it too, but I now knew I had to do something about it. But how?

Meanwhile, college life continued. Teaching practices, three in all, spread over the duration of the course, looked like a behind the scenes view of *Blue Peter* – 'here's one I made earlier', stage by stage artwork to demonstrate my ideas to the class, work sheets showing exactly what I required of them and a white board and marker pen which I somehow managed to write on more successfully than a blackboard with chalk. I had teams of markers to sit alongside me and wade through the usual sixty to ninety exercise books a night and many Braille records to keep of each child's progress. It was a steep learning curve for me and involved much trial and error as I was told I was the first blind primary school teacher in the country and thus had no one to advise me.

Visits by external examiners to view progress of students in school were supposed to be a purely random choice by the examination board; it seemed rather suspicious to me that throughout the three years my name would always appear on the lists. The pressure in college to succeed, both in the practical teaching and also in the general college course work, was great.

For the final college music practical, I was required to give a recital lasting an hour and a half. This would include my piano, voice, recorder and guitar studies along with a performance from the girls' choir I had trained over the past few years. We were required to attain grade eight in two instruments and seven in a third. The recorder, both treble and sopranino, along with voice was a much easier task with only one line of music to learn. Classical guitar and piano were a much greater challenge. I had the benefit of some wonderful and patient teachers who would pains-takingly work through just a few bars of music, over and over again each week, recording them on tape for me to use when practising. Week by week I would add another line of music to Beethoven's Moonlight Sonata, Romanza and numbers of other pieces in my repertoire until finally, with joy and relief, the final bars would be added. Although this method was slow and required much determination I would at least end up with pieces that needed no work on correcting mistakes as they had all been ironed out along the way. The recital itself, though nerve-wracking as I stretched my memory capacity to the full, was a success. It was a relief to know, as I turned my attention to the remainder of the academic exams and practical assess-ments, that I no longer needed to retain this huge bank of music in my memory.

Towards the end of my third and final year I was assigned to St Edward's Primary School for my third, six week long, teaching practice. The reality of working in a classroom on a daily basis, the mountains of prepara-tion that it entailed and the vast quantity of daily written preparation necessary for the college tutors caused mount-ing pressure. My desire to succeed coupled with my love for teaching began to be buried under the strain of external examination and the unmistakable message from many of those in authority of my expected failure. Things came to a head on the fourth weekend.

'I can't do this, Peter,' I began to sob. 'I just can't do this. It's too much. I'm so tired and they all think I'm going to fail.'

Peter wrapped his arms around me and held me close. 'You're not going to fail, look how far you've come. It's going to be all right; just two more weeks. You can do it.'

I looked up at him. 'Sorry.' I sniffed. 'Sometimes I just long to be able to see; it's so hard.' I snuggled into him again. 'I love you.'

It was with great relief therefore, that my teaching practice ended successfully and the final exams produced a high qualification: necessary to prove my capability as a classroom teacher, as a low pass mark would have undoubtedly put a question mark over my teaching ability.

Soon I was employed as a probationary teacher in a nearby town. It was in a very deprived part of the county and my class comprised thirty-six seven and eight year olds from mixed cultures and backgrounds. They were all a delight to me, if not a mixed bag of personalities. From some tough family backgrounds, their supposed hardness melted away as they came for a surreptitious cuddle at play times – once their friends had left the classroom, of course. Some little girls rushed in late for school on a regular basis, flustered and excusing themselves.

'I'm sorry I'm late, Miss, I had to go and buy bacon and cigarettes for my dad before school and then take my little brother to the infants on the way.'

'That's all right, Tina,' I smiled. What a life – only seven and with the responsibilities of the household on her little shoulders.

Many families had a number of their older children in prison; and many of the boys at school were regularly visited by the police, the day after they had been made to climb through small windows at night in order for their older brothers to break into properties. I had a great love for these children, beginning their lives in such a difficult manner, on a path which looked like repeating itself, handed down from generation to generation. I knew nothing then of the God who could deliver them from such a life, not necessarily removing them from their circumstances, but giving them a new hope and joy and a purpose for living to prepare the way for their own children.

I was blessed with Mr Walker, a head teacher who believed that I could teach. This was not always the case as I was told on a number of occasions very emphatically, by some college tutors and one educational advisor, that 'blind people can't teach'. I invited them to come and observe me teaching, though the thought of them coming filled me with nervousness; but it seemed the only way of proving myself. However, they declined my offers as they had already made up their minds. Mr Walker, though, was a wonderful man with an open heart and mind and would make his own opinion based on what he saw for himself. He was prepared to back me as other members of staff were concerned about the possibility of having to take on added responsibilities because of me. However, when they found that I was offering to take their dreaded music periods in exchange for their beloved PE and games, which, for insurance purposes, was the only subject I was not allowed to take, their anxieties were removed.

I thoroughly enjoyed my time there and learned to live under the expected pressure of having to make sure that my class was the best behaved, with the best of wall displays, producing excellent written work and exam results, in order to quash my anticipated failure as a blind teacher. My lovely guide-dog, Solo, sat contentedly under my desk throughout the day and I firmly believe that, within a week, the children forgot that they had a blind teacher. They would happily come out brandishing their latest painting or drawing under my nose.

'Do you like it, Miss?' they would ask, enthusiastically waving it around.

'It's super. Tell me all about it.' They would then go off into great verbal detail, laying out the picture in my mind.

'How about putting in some flowers at the bottom edge?' I'd suggest.

'Ooh yes, blue and pink would look nice!'

'Off you go, then.'

It was easy. I adopted the same method with reading books, written stories and maths problems. Inevitably by the time they had explained only half of their difficulty, they suddenly realised the solutions for themselves without me needing to tell them. This encouraged their own thinking instead of relying on 'teacher' to give out the answers. Discipline and strict routine were essential for my success, but we also had many lovely moments as they not only came to me for their daily cuddle but also to stroke the dog.

There was only one parent who was determined to prove that her daughter was suffering in her education due to having a blind teacher. She made a complaint to Mr Walker that I had put Jane on a reading book level far below her capability. As I stood in the headmaster's room, quaking with fear, she exclaimed,

'Jane reads *The Times* newspaper at home. You obviously aren't capable of doing your job correctly. My sister is a teacher, I know about these things.'

Mr Walker stepped in, cutting short her verbal aggression towards me.

'I'm sure Miss Lawson can show you her records marking her testing and progress. Would you like to go and bring them here, Miss Lawson?'

I picked up Solo's harness, fingers trembling, and left the room. I could hear her voice, high pitched and insistent as I made my way back to the classroom. All those hours of painstakingly keeping Braille records were now worthwhile. I returned and read out her daughter's progress report. Her daughter was summoned and asked to read her present book, far simpler than *The Times*.

Jane steadily read her way down the page, hesitating over some more difficult words as I helped her to spell them out and pronounce them.

'I think we can see that Miss Lawson has clearly assessed your daughter correctly,' said Mr Walker. 'That will be all Miss Lawson, thank you.'

Relief flooded over me and a great sense of elation that my first hurdle of parental prejudice had been overcome, but with it came the realisation that there would always be people with preconceived ideas about my capabilities and that I would need to maintain excellence in all I did in order to safeguard myself.

Peter and I had become engaged in the autumn and six months later, on 5th April 1980, at Nunthorpe Methodist Church, we married. It was a gloriously sunny day despite having snowed two days previously. Family and friends celebrated with us. I had inherited a ready made family as Peter had a brother, Geoff, and three lovely sisters, June, Hazel and Carole. We would all be married and have children in the years to come, spending some lovely times together in each other's homes during the holidays.

Our wedding took place on Easter Saturday, which gave us a further week away from school to spend three wonderful days on honeymoon in the Lake District. I changed from a 'Miss' to a 'Mrs' during that school break and both my class and myself took some time to get used to this change! We were very fortunate to be able to buy a semi-detached house in which to begin our married life together as, although I was teaching, Peter was still in his final year at college.

So far, I had spent my whole life as a northern lass. I knew my way around the area and had all the surrounding sights firmly in my mind. I had no desire to leave this area. With its beautiful moorlands stretching as far as the eye could see, its peace and tranquillity, wildlife, raw weather

Our wedding day, 5th April 1980

and some of the friendliest people you could ever hope to meet, this was home and my new husband, thankfully, loved it.

After my time at Westbury Street Primary, I moved on to another school where the children came from similar backgrounds and, by now, was into the swing of teaching and Braille record keeping. The children brought me a lot of joy and I anticipated a lifelong career as a schoolteacher whenever thinking of my future.

FOUR

From Heights to Depths

As the weeks went by I began to feel quite ill, far more weary than was usual with rheumatoid arthritis, which continued to make me become extremely tired. As each day wore on, I had a real desperate feeling about me and felt most uncomfortable inside. The thought crossed my mind that perhaps I was pregnant; it seemed very soon but I made an appointment with my GP.

'What can I do for you?' he asked.

'I think I might be expecting a baby,' I proffered.

'How long have you been married now?' he asked

'Only a couple of months.' He told me that with my general condition and the long-term medication I was taking it wasn't likely.

'It will just be all the changes in your life and the teaching job, too. Just go home, get on with things and don't be a silly girl.'

' "A silly girl," he called me a silly girl, Peter,' I said with tears in my eyes. 'If it's not that then what is it? I feel so terrible, so very ill.'

A few more weeks went by but I only felt worse. I believed what doctors told me, so if I wasn't pregnant then I must have something seriously wrong with me. I became extremely worried and frightened and thoughts of yet more hospitalisation began to plague my mind. In desperation we contacted a local minister, who we heard had something to do with healing – something we knew nothing about – but when desperate any straw to clutch at will do, especially, in my case, if it avoided visiting the doctor again.

'He has no space to see us until later next week,' Peter told me as he came back into the bedroom.

'Next week!' I burst into tears. 'I need to see him now – I can't go on like this.'

'I'm so sorry Kate, I tried but we'll just have to wait. It will be all right.' He held me tightly and I took strength from his reassurance.

By the time we went to his home, I would have done anything to receive peace in my life. He showed us into his large sitting room and left us together for a short while. It was so peaceful there. An aquarium bubbled gently across the room and a grandfather clock, with its deep ticking, seemed to meter my breathing and thoughts. We just sat there, not daring to even whisper. I wondered what exactly I was doing there, now it had come to the crunch. The minister returned and spoke to us both and then asked if Peter would mind going into his other sitting room. Now I was alone.

I don't recall exactly what he said to me, something about the cross and Christ crucified, something about the power of the Holy Spirit and much about others he knew who had given their lives to Jesus Christ. I surrendered my life then and there; there was no other option. At last, with relief, I had within me what I had been searching for. A wonderful peace came into my life. I felt held by love, enveloped by warmth and filled with amazing courage and hope. I had no idea what had happened but only knew that all would be well. I knew nothing, in fact, of what would be the consequence or effect on my life due to such a decision.

As we left for home, I was overwhelmed by the need to put things right in my life, and a relationship between a neighbouring family and ourselves that had turned quite bitter preyed on my mind. To Peter's horror, I insisted that I go to their home there and then, and put matters right. We rang the doorbell and were met with much surprise but invited in nevertheless. We sat down facing the whole family and, to the best of my ability, I tried to explain what had happened to me that night and to say that I was sorry for what had happened between our families. I asked them to forgive me for my part, but there was no response.

After a few moments of silence, I got up and we left, thanking them for their time. As the front door closed behind us I heard great laughter and jeering words on the night air. Somehow, they didn't hurt me as before. I was learning, without realising it, the Lord's need and desire for us to repent of those things in our past, to put them right and to forgive those who have hurt us, regardless of their response.

We continued on our way home and to bed. It was a short time later that the heat in my body increased and I became aware that 'Someone' was in our room. I opened my eyes and there He stood – Jesus – by my bedside, ema- nating such a white light that I could see His form quite clearly, despite my lack of sight. 'Peace,' He said. That was all I needed to hear. 'He's here,' I whispered to Peter and then wave upon wave of tranquillity washed through and over me. I felt a great lightness in my body and began to pray in a whisper for what seemed like hours to this won- derful Jesus who had met with me, pouring out my heart in words which were totally foreign to me.

Peter was, I remember, astonished by this and kept leaning over me with his ear against my mouth. He never asked me what was happening, as we both sensed the awesomeness of the presence of God. That night, without knowing it, was the opening of the door in my life to the power of the Holy Spirit, a gift from God to enable us all to accomplish the work set before each one of us: 'For we are His workmanship, created in Christ Jesus for good works, which God prepared beforehand, that we should walk in them' (Ephesians 2:10). It was to be many years before I encountered this power again but God does not let us go; even though we may lose sight of Him, willingly or unwillingly, He pursues us, as a Shepherd after His sheep.

Some weeks later, I noticed that my clothes were becoming tighter and the original seed of a thought came back to me – could I really be expecting a baby? I became more anxious as time went by and I began to feel more and more poorly. We decided to take matters into our own hands and bought a home test. To our delight and astonishment it confirmed that I was indeed going to have a baby. Returning to my rather surprised GP with the news I began the rounds of the maternity hospital, clinics and specialists.

Peter became more and more apprehensive every time I went for my fortnightly check up as, on each return home, the date for the birth rapidly reduced a month or more, and so my nine month pregnancy became only four months! During this time, my love for the Lord Jesus grew and my relationship with Him as Saviour, a Friend who was now very much alive to me, increased. My trust in Him was about to be tested; with the imminent birth of my baby I was about to learn to lean on Him even more.

Born on 12th February 1981, a beautiful dark haired little girl, Rebecca Katherine, weighing six pounds, six ounces. After the usual checks, we were told that she had a double dislocation of the hips. It caused us no real upset at the time as we were assured this was not such an unusual occurrence and would soon clear up with the use of double nappies. We were wonderfully happy and content.

How wrong the hospital were with their prognosis,

however. We were to undertake two years of hospital visits, operations, plastercast changes. It was an upsetting time as I watched my beautiful little baby disappear off to the operating theatre and observed various treatments and procedures cause her distress.

I, sadly, received much discouragement from many professionals around me who told me that, as a blind mum, I would never cope. The incredulous voice of the health visitor asked, 'Do you manage to dress her yourself?'

I secretly longed to reply, 'No, I leave her lying naked all day until my husband comes home to do it for me.' Thankfully, the grace of God in my life enabled me to keep my mouth closed.

Then there were the insensitive comments of others:

'Oh, she's so beautiful and you can't see her.'

'I expect your mum comes round most of the time to do everything for you.'

I fought a daily battle with the misconceptions which the 'blind' label brings whilst at the same time learning to cope with the inner wounds of thoughtless but nevertheless hurtful remarks which began, without my realisation, to erode my self-worth. However, I had a strength within me far greater than all of my circumstances – Jesus Christ. My faith in Him began to grow. I spent many hours each day talking and singing to Rebecca, describing things around the house, even though I couldn't see them for myself, preparing food and feeding her as she moved onto solids, and generally extending my housekeeping skills. God was with me and on one day in particular, His ability to save us from any and every situation was tested to the full.

I had fed Rebecca and put her down in her carrycot. As soon as she had dropped off to sleep, I took the washing in my laundry basket out into the garden, through the side gate, to hang it out in the sunshine. The job done, I returned to the side gate but to my utter horror and then rising panic, it seemed to be stuck fast. I went back to it a number of times, pushing and banging but to no avail. I was so aware of my little baby alone in the house and of the fact that no one was due home for many hours. I didn't know what to do. I stood in the middle of the lawn, the washing flapping in the breeze above my head and prayed, 'Please help me Jesus, I need to get to Rebecca before she wakes up.' Then, with no other option, I headed for the dividing fence that separated us from our neighbour's garden.

I still don't know how I managed to climb over the fence, but I found myself at the other side.

'Please don't let me fall into a pond or anything,' I whispered.

I moved tentatively forward, heading towards their house with the mirror image of our own home in my mind. His strength was upon me, His courage welled up within me and His guiding hand led me on. I found the back of the house and followed the wall around to the front and then, hoping that no one was watching me, I kept my hand against the warm bricks as I traced my route past their front door and window.

I kept up my conversation as my heart raced, 'Oh, don't let there be a dividing fence at the front.'

There wasn't; I soon found our front door and, now on familiar ground, headed down the drive and entered the back door. As I picked up my baby, I thanked Him for His amazing empowering love towards me.

When Peter returned that evening from work, he was astonished to hear my tale. We went out to inspect the side gate. It opened easily. We stood in the garden, puzzled, then he realised what had happened. In my haste to return to the house I had mistakenly gone to the side door of the garage, which was always locked firmly. My bearings lost I had returned again and again to the wrong gate. All that unnecessary anxiety – but now, I knew even more that, as

I had read in His Word, 'I can do all things through Him who strengthens me' (Philippians 4:13).

By this time we were involved in our local United Reformed church, and working with the youth group, which comprised many differing characters whose ages ranged from twelve to eighteen. We spent many extremely happy hours with these young people. They filled our, now, little bungalow (a necessary move due to the cumbersome and weighty plasters Rebecca was encased in from waist to ankle. This caused my joints much distress as I carried her up and down the stairs and climbed in and out of the back seat of our Mini car). Most evenings and weekends were filled with various events – horse riding, bowling, swimming; burger and video nights. These were all surrounded with worship and Bible studies. As a group we took whole youth services, surprising the congregation with guitars, harmonies and some hilarious dramas, spurred on by a contemporary magazine, at that time called *Buzz*.

We opened our home four evenings a week, two to accommodate the youth and the remainder for house groups, which were formed after the Billy Graham Mission England visit to the then Roker Park football ground, Sunderland. I had a busy but satisfying time co-ordinating the buses from our area for the Mission week and sorting out the follow-up visits and aftercare. It was a wonderful time of learning and meeting for the first time those who were in great need of our Saviour, Jesus. Many of our youth group came to know Jesus during that week of mission as did numbers of our church congregation. It was an awesome time as the Holy Spirit convicted hundreds each night to come to the front and give their lives to Christ. It was the silence during the response to Jesus that struck me most, a silence only broken by the erratic sound of stadium seats tipping up and the quiet tread of feet making their way along the walkways leading onto the turf.

Our house groups usually comprised around fifteen people each evening. We had some amazing times together, studying the Bible and worshipping. I clearly recall one evening in particular when Lucy, a young lady who had recently become a Christian, began to sniff the air.

'Can you smell something?' she enquired of the room in general, 'something beautiful?'

'What kind of smell?' we replied.

'Like perfume,' she answered.

What a scene! We crowded around her space and sniffed the air as she was so certain and becoming excited, desperate for us to share in her experience. Then we realised, with awed quietness, it was the perfume of the Lord we had read about in His Word (*see* Exodus 30:22-25; the name 'Christ' means 'Anointed One'). He was giving Lucy a tangible sign of His presence amongst us. We sat for a long time drinking it in. Our experience of the manifestations of God's presence in our lives was beginning to widen, though at the time we had no idea what was to come.

Four years on from the birth of our daughter, Rebecca, we once again found ourselves excitedly expecting another baby. Secretly we hoped for another girl but openly said nothing; we prayed for a healthy baby and on 27th July 1985 our gorgeous daughter, Victoria Kate, was born. Beautiful black hair and amazingly long legs, our secret prayer answered – two beautiful daughters – treasures from God to bring up as best we could in His nurture, two treasures who would bring us both the greatest of joy and delight as the years moved on.

My body, unlike my mind and emotions, however, was not in line with my feelings of contentment. The arthritis, which seemed to abate during pregnancy, much to my delight, came back suddenly with a vengeance, a few weeks after Victoria's birth. One Sunday lunchtime, arriving home after church, I discovered that I had great difficulty in getting out of the car. We had a narrow drive and my passenger door only opened up to half its normal width. I removed my seat belt, opened the door and turned to get out. As I went to bend my legs in order to squeeze through the gap a jarring pain hit my knees.

'I can't bend my knees properly,' I exclaimed, dropping back into my seat. I looked ahead not wanting to face Peter. It was happening again, the arthritis – surely it couldn't be returning? Peter touched my shoulder; he always knew what I was thinking.

'It's all right; I'll come round and hold the door open for you.'

With a struggle I stood up. As I made my way around the car towards the house I knew the worst had happened. Rebecca was chattering away, rushing on ahead as usual, Peter lifting Victoria from her car seat, and as I struggled up the three steps to the front door, heaving myself up with the use of the handrail, my knees froze up into a once familiar position and the pain began to return.

Within weeks my joint situation had deteriorated. It seemed, according to the doctors, that during the time of carrying a baby the rise in certain naturally made substances would have lubricated my joints, but as soon as the birth was over, all that natural chemical would have left my body. Now, not only were my knee joints affected, but to my horror, every joint in my body began to follow suit, throbbing with the most appalling pain. There was no relief day or night; no amount of pain killers could touch it.

In desperation for a solution I turned to a local homeopath, recommended to me by a number of people who had seemingly found an answer for their so far unsolved aches and pains. He was a lovely man who talked at length about my illnesses and asked general questions about my life. He then prescribed a remedy. I took it – I would have taken or done anything he recommended in order to be free of my present situation. Within a matter of weeks, just before Christmas, I became dreadfully ill.

Christmas morning arrived and our excited daughter, Rebecca, crept into the living room with us to see if Father Christmas had been. Sure enough, there were the two stockings, hanging either side of the fireplace, filled to the brim, a chocolate Santa peering over the top. Only the coloured fairy lights on the tree lit our room and, with carols playing in the background, we had an exciting half hour as Rebecca dug deep into her stocking, producing a bottle of bubbles, a pen with a snowman on the top, a bag of chocolate money and right down in the toe, a satsuma.

As I sat there in my dressing gown listening to excited shouts of joy and the frantic tearing of wrapping paper mingled with gurgles of delight from Victoria, lying contentedly in her baby chair, the throbbing in my body continued relentlessly. I became aware of the tree lights, no longer, it seemed, giving a gentle glow to the room but somehow penetrating into my head. I kept this to myself, for this was no day to give in to illness.

We dressed in our best clothes, piled into the car and set off to my parents' home where we were invited for Christmas dinner. We arrived just on time and I sat at the table, pulled the obligatory cracker, laughed and groaned at the jokes found inside and placed my hat on my head. I fixed my smile like a beauty queen but things were going really wrong inside me. By the time I faced my dinner plate I knew I couldn't eat. My mouth didn't want to work and my throat refused to swallow. I forced down a teaspoon's worth of mashed potato and gave up. We kept up a good front for Rebecca's sake and then, as Victoria made her need known for her own brand of festive food, I struggled up from the table and went to sit in a comfortable armchair. Peter placed Victoria on my lap and I laid her head on my right elbow in order to feed her. Her beautiful tiny head nestled into the crook of my arm but even such a light weight as that caused me to cry out with pain.

'It's so awful Peter, I want to go on holding her for hours but I just can't.'

My tears fell as she finished her feed and I had to relinquish my hold to Peter in the hope of some pain relief for my arms.

As soon as the holiday period was over I contacted my homeopath and more remedies were prescribed, including it seemed, the necessity to exclude certain foods, as they would apparently hinder the effectiveness of the tablets. I had no idea at the time that these initial food exclusions would escalate into an eating disorder, which would last for many years to come. I became totally dependent on this man and his remedies, carrying bottles of them with me wherever I went, believing that he had the answer for me; he believed it too. Without realising it, homeopathy in general, this man and his remedies in particular, had become in my life what the Bible calls 'an idol', a false god, causing me to break the first commandment: 'You shall have no other gods before me' (Exodus 20:2). Instead of turning to Jesus as my first source of healing and comfort, I would rush to the phone for guidance, turn to my book of remedies and never leave the house without my handbag full of tablets.

As time went by and the pain and lack of mobility increased I became more and more frustrated with my body and greatly depressed. However, having been brought up with a very positive way of thinking, I rejected the whole idea of 'being depressed,' even though I had read that this was a quite common event after the birth of a baby and could be easily treated. With so much happening to me, this particular reason for my turmoil never occurred to me. All my energy was spent trying to push away the feelings of misery and fear that rose up in me each morning as I awoke, feelings which would remain with me throughout the day and in the many hours I lay awake at night, too. I felt so guilty – I had the most wonderful gentle, kind and loving husband, two beautiful, funny and charming daughters of whom I was so proud, a beautiful home, a car, holidays abroad. What was wrong with me? I hated the seeming ungratefulness in me and the sense of being a failure, both as a wife and mother and, of course, wasn't I supposed to be a 'victorious Christian,' too?

Because of my physical problems, now finding even the shortest distance to walk impossible, I began to stay in the house more often. Occasional trips out on a Saturday to the shops consisted of spraying pain relief spray to numb the joints of my legs in order for me to walk around for an hour or so. The resulting consequence of yet more pain from my efforts to spend time out of the house became too much to cope with and so I found myself becoming trapped in my own home. Aware of every touch on my joints from those around me, furniture, cutlery and even bedcovers, coupled with an inability to see, my depression increased.

After a year of struggling with mounting feelings of drowning in my situation, I approached Christmas with a great sense of eagerness for a really happy family cel-ebration. It was such a favourite time of year for us; we had already a number of traditions built into this time. Decorating the tree together signalled the beginning of Christmas in our home. The daily excitement of opening the doors on the advent calendar increased our anticipa-tion of the day itself. There was of course much food prep-aration: baking mince pies, watching over the children as they stuffed dates with marzipan and excitedly stirring the Christmas pudding before cooking it slowly overnight to ensure a rich, sumptuous, dark pudding.

On Christmas Eve we would read the nativity story by

candlelight and pray together, thanking Jesus for coming to this earth for us. Just before bed the children would excitedly hang up their stockings either side of the fireplace, leaving out a mince pie and cup of milk for Father Christmas along with the obligatory carrot for Rudolph.

The final Christmas Eve shopping trip with my mum to the local supermarket triggered the first massive panic attack, a totally unexpected shock which gripped my mind and emotions and rendered my body exhausted. Fears of the present and for the future seized my mind as I stumbled on, holding everything together on the outside for all to see whilst inside I was falling deeper and deeper into a dark hole.

I pressed on with daily family life; the joy of having my beautiful baby daughter to look after, my bubbly elder daughter who brought the house alive with her giggles and chatter, the daily routine of housework and all that entailed, and the pleasure of watching both my little girls play together after school. Rebecca was devoted to her little sister, always protecting her and telling everyone just how beautiful she was.

We spent many wonderfully happy hours together, playing shops, cooking, painting, dancing and singing to the piano and listening to favourite stories on cassette, like *The Ugly Duckling* and *The Gingerbread Man*. I learned Victoria's favourite books off by heart – *The Very Hungry Caterpillar*, *Pelican* and *Burglar Bill*, to name only a few. We spent many hours singing and dancing along to music tapes of Psalty, a walking, talking songbook who taught about the love of Jesus, and Marilyn Baker records, whose Bible truths in rhythmical tunes were ideal for this. It became apparent that we were beginning to outgrow our little bungalow and that we needed to look for something bigger. The girls were sharing a bedroom now which caused much hilarity at bedtimes, though Rebecca became

Rebecca and six-week-old Victoria on our family holiday, 1985

an expert in telling made up Rascally Rabbit stories to Victoria to help her 'stay in her bed' until sleep overcame her.

Three months later, in April 1988, we celebrated the Easter school holiday with a move into a 1930s semi-detached house in an older part of our town. It had a lovely large side garden with three huge trees and, with a small breakfast room next to the kitchen, we could use the dining room as a music room. It was ideal for family music times but it was also spacious enough for the church worship group practice, which Peter now led. However, this move was to prove a major event in my life which none of us could have foreseen. This beautiful old house was to become my downfall, which would lead to many 'wilderness years'. And so the words of Psalm 23, learned in junior school many years earlier, became a reality in my life: 'Even though I walk through the valley of the shadow of death . . .' (Psalm 23:4).

That first night in our new home further catapulted me into a three day collapse, triggered by the noise of traffic during the night. It was during the stay in my parents' home that the encouraging words from my dad to 'just be myself and choose whatever I wanted' were to plant a seed which God took, I believe, and began to make me desire to be 'myself' – the woman God had always intended me to be, the woman He had created and chosen for His purposes. This is the case for each one of us, uniquely created, knit together in our mother's womb, the Bible tells us, created for a specific plan and purpose. We are not a random happening or a mistake. Both you and I were specifically created for a very special and particular time on this earth. When we invite Jesus to come into our lives and allow Him to bring us into His plans and purposes for us, we will find fullness of life, peace and great joy.

The fourth morning of my enforced stay saw me up and dressed, my willpower once again in place and a determination to succeed despite the situation. We returned to our new home and continued unpacking boxes but I was acutely aware of the traffic going to and fro outside the house. This included buses and lorries causing not only engine noise but vibrations in the house as well. The night time loomed and once again we went to bed but there was no escape into sleep for me. Again I paced the floors, retiring exhausted to bed as dawn rose, but sleep would not come. This cycle went on for some time, snatching a few hours here and there, but the noise in my ears dogged me day and night. I would lie in bed willing myself to sleep and dropping into bouts of great despair.

This was our home, our choice, we loved it, but for me

it was a nightmare. How was I to tell Peter how I felt? We had sold up and were settled in. We couldn't move again, that was ridiculous, but how could I live with this noise and the lack of sleep . . . why did no one else notice it as I did? I began to fear the future; it stretched out before me, exhausting, dark and lonely. I lay awake in the night feeling that the whole world was asleep except for me and the longing to be away from all of this began to take over my thoughts.

I was a failure. I couldn't cope with something simple like a bit of traffic noise. My weariness began to affect everything else. I got things wrong when preparing meals and doing the most trivial of household tasks. I became clumsy and couldn't concentrate properly anymore. I cried out to God for help but He didn't seem to hear. No one could help me, I was in this alone or so it felt. My lack of self-worth began to increase and I moved even deeper into depression.

It was like a dark hole; once I began to drop down there seemed no way of climbing back up again. No matter how much I wanted to, it was impossible. The blackness surrounded me, swamped every hopeful thought and replaced confidence with fear, light with dark and love with a desire to tear down. These feelings and thoughts were horrifying to me. It was as if I stood outside of myself, watching and listening, helpless to stop myself thinking and speaking, acting and reacting the way I was. Appalled by all of this, I began to dislike myself and what I felt I stood for – everything that was wrong.

Over the next few years I attempted to keep my life together. Amazingly I continued teaching part-time in a primary school for three afternoons a week. Having said goodbye to Peter, I would get the girls off to school, all smart in their uniforms, clutching their bags and packed lunches. After tidying up the breakfast pots and feeding my new guide-dog, Axel, I would go back to bed for an hour's sleep, setting the alarm clock for eleven thirty, giving me enough time to eat lunch and travel to the school. This short sleep was to give me the strength I needed to cope with a classroom of lively children, return home to prepare the evening meal and enjoy many hours of fun and games with the girls before bed.

Summer holidays were a great psychological challenge. I loved the idea of being away with the family but as the time to leave came near the panic would once again rise in me. Somehow I managed to fight off my fears during the day, the girls keeping my mind on other things. We had wonderful family times visiting farms, country fairs, baking fresh pies from blackberries picked by the girls, walks in the rain and trips on boats and trains.

We had a major holiday in Switzerland along with both grandmothers. I focused on getting there and made it. Though exhausted, the beauty of the surroundings was worth it and the excitement of the girls at all they saw spurred me on. However, as the days went by I began once more to struggle with outings. After one week on a beautiful sunny afternoon as we sat by Lake Brienz, I had an overwhelming feeling of panic and had to return to our chalet with Peter, leaving the girls to return later with the grandmas. I sat in the bedroom by the open wooden shutters with the sunshine sparkling on the snow topped mountain view, wondering how I was going to make it home again. It was so far away.

Peter's mum returned and came into the room. 'Are you all right, Kate?' she queried.

I turned to her, tears streaming down my face. There were no words to express the feelings within me. She held me close. She was so loving and kind, sensing my desperation. 'It's all right, sweetheart,' she said, 'it's going to be all right.'

I gathered my inner resources once more, pushing the return journey from my mind, determined to enjoy the remainder of the holiday. Sometimes, sitting in a pedalo on the lake with Rebecca and Victoria splashing water over me, sitting on the chair lifts as we glided effortlessly to the tops of mountains, holding tight to the girls' hands as we chugged up the mountain railway, it was hard to imagine that there was anything wrong. The journey home, three days by road, proved otherwise however. I sat in the front seat of the car, looking steadfastly ahead for the whole of the journey, willing myself to make it. I did, of course, though that was always the greatest fear, that somehow I wouldn't.

I know now that the grace and mercy of God was upon me but during that time I felt it to be a lone fight, despite the love, care and encouragement of my devoted husband and the great joy my beautiful daughters brought me. Life sometimes seemed like climbing a physical mountain, riding an emotional roller coaster, often plummeting me down to ground level and sometimes, it seemed, below. It was often a time of mental torture and great despair.

The guilt I felt was overwhelming; there was I, a young woman with a wonderfully kind and loving husband, two beautiful, healthy, funny, full-of-life daughters, a good loving extended family on both sides, a beautiful home, car, good income, holidays, clothes, food . . . what else did I need, how ungrateful was I? The sense of being a failed wife, mother and Christian was indeed too great to bear at times. I know now, of course, that condemnation and guilt never comes from God ('There is therefore now no condemnation for those who are in Christ Jesus . . .' Romans 8:1), only from the enemy, but this revelation was to be given to me in years to come. I had, without realising, given the devil 'a foothold' (Ephesians 4.27 NIV) and he had taken full advantage of it.

I looked around for a solution. I felt I was a burden, a nuisance and my whole life must only be bringing hurt and pain to Peter, who, in my eyes, bore the whole of my struggle. However, I had left the central person out of my thinking and that was Jesus Christ Himself. His Word tells us, 'I will never leave you nor forsake you' (Hebrews 13:5), but by now my eyes and ears were blinded to the truth. Thankfully, unbeknown to me as I was well beyond listening to any words of hope, Peter held on to his small seed of faith, encouraging himself with the words of Psalm 27, which he kept with him: 'I know that I will live to see the LORD's goodness in this present life. Trust in the LORD. Have faith, do not despair. Trust in the LORD' (Psalm 27:13-14).

One day Peter went walking and climbed Roseberry Topping, a local point in the Cleveland Hills. He sat on a rock overlooking the beautiful countryside and wept. He had come to the realisation that there was nothing else he could do to change the situation and so cried out to the Lord for His help.

'Oh God, I feel so useless; please do something. There's nothing more I can do to help her, I've tried everything. I love her so much but I've reached the end. I give her to you, Lord.'

In my humanness, there were two solutions to my situation. I vacillated from one to the other in a desperate desire to solve the problem of living. During the days when the darkest of despair would swamp both my mind and emotions I would find myself standing at the top of the stairs, imagining myself lying at the bottom and then being found, by whom I didn't care, but something deep inside me yearned for help. I felt that if my situation became serious enough then somehow this empty hole in me would be filled.

Thoughts of self-hatred would bombard my mind. I would be making a cup of tea and want to pour the hot water over my hands in order to punish myself for my perceived failure in life, believing by doing this that it would relieve my pain. Sometimes the frustration of my situation was so great that a small and, seemingly irrelevant, situation would magnify itself in my mind to such a degree that I would pick up the nearest objects and hurl them around. Only when on my own or when Peter was about did I ever allow these frustrations to come out into the open. I could not let my lovely daughters see their mummy behaving in such a way, I loved them so much.

I recall one morning in particular, whilst preparing breakfast for the family, not being able to find a bowl I had left on the kitchen work surface. I lost control, picked up a large, full box of cornflakes and began to scatter them everywhere around the kitchen, eventually hurling the box to the ground and bursting into the inevitable flood of tears and regret as Peter held me in his arms.

'It's all right, its going to be all right; I love you so much,' he murmured into my ear.

The other side of my solution was to find activities that were beyond the norm for a visually impaired person; it would give me a thrill, the adrenalin rush and sense of 'being someone important', that sense of being accepted and special. I heard of a gentleman with a Rolls Royce who was willing for a disabled person to drive it, so I contacted him and within a few weeks, there I was on a racetrack at the wheel of a gold Rolls Royce. The press were there, unbeknown to me at his request, along with the champagne. The build up to this had filled the gap temporarily as I had taken a number of driving lessons at a local racetrack.

Speeding along at around seventy miles per hour was really exhilarating for me. I looked forward with eager anticipation at taking the wheel of such an amazing car. However, it ended in disappointment as the speed of the car was the crucial part for me. It was only as I switched on the ignition that I discovered he had placed a wood block under the accelerator and the maximum speed was to be only thirty miles per hour. I felt such a fool crawling round the circuit and I guessed the owner was just after some publicity for his business.

I also entered a driving competition, or at least my daughters entered me, at the Middlesbrough Guide-dog Centre open day. After successfully, in the shortest time, manoeuvring my way around a slalom course with a co-driver giving me verbal instructions, I became the proud and amused owner of a plaque displaying the words 'Woman Driver of the Year'. I contacted a national radio station too, suggesting it would make a good story to have me drive a racing car at Brands Hatch. They agreed, much to my amazement, and some weeks later the letter arrived with the date of the event. Before I was to take the wheel yet again, however, God was about to intervene in such a way that I wrote and declined their offer, apologising for the time I had wasted but giving them my reasons for pulling out – I didn't need to do this any more.

FIVE

And Suddenly . . .

Friday evenings were the most difficult night of the week for me. Worship practice was held in our home and, having got the girls to bed each week, I would hear the approaching cars on the drive and go and hide away in our bedroom, only coming downstairs a couple of hours later when they had all left. I would sit on the bed hearing the music, wishing I could join in but knowing that without being able to read the music it was hopeless. I didn't even know these people as this was the new church plant in our area, where Peter led the worship group. Services were originally held in a room of the local pub, complete with parrot who would sit amiably on the shoulders of those praying together before the service began. They had acquired the community centre in recent weeks and were now able to expand the group, bringing in a pianist to complement the guitars and other instruments.

These evenings gave me a distant longing to be a part of it all and for a brief moment my will power rose up and I voiced my desire to God.

'I'd love to be back in church again but I can't do it.' My mind ran back to past years.

'I must do it, but how? In the new year I will take all my courage in both hands and make myself go.'

I was so afraid though, I didn't know anyone there or what they would think of me. What if I had a panic attack, what if I let Peter down? The Bible tells us that God wants to give us the desires of our heart (Psalm 37:4); how could He ever manage this desire? Had He even heard me? It was only a brief moment of desire, I hardly dared think about it as it became an enormous mountain in my mind. I didn't ask Him to help me, I couldn't – it had been too long since I had asked Him for anything. I didn't want to risk Him not answering me, not helping me, because then I would know that what I had feared was true – that no one, not even God Himself, could rescue me from this pit of hopelessness.

The first Friday in January 1992 arrived, just like any other Friday worship practice. They came; I hid. Eventually I heard them all chatting in the hall as they donned coats to leave and then peace descended; time to go downstairs. As I reached the halfway point on the staircase, to my horror a man's voice spoke from below.

'Hello Kate, nice to meet you.'

I was shocked: he must have been in the music room whilst the others left, and then, to my even greater dismay and shock, I heard my own voice.

'Would you like to stay for a cup of tea?'

What was I doing? I felt my face flush with panic; my heart began to thump in my chest, my mind raced ahead . . . they had already all had a drink; surely he would refuse?

But he accepted with great pleasure in his voice, 'That would be lovely, thank you.'

Peter, also somewhat amazed at my invitation, showed him into the front sitting room. I made my way down the remainder of the stairs hoping Peter would come out to me and would help me to get rid of this man, but he didn't. I found myself making tea, setting a tray and running through a plan of action in my mind. If I just went in, put down the tray and stayed standing, I could quickly give my apologies and leave the room. It would be all right, I could do it without appearing rude.

So, carrying the tea tray, I pushed open the front room door and, as I did so, the gentleman said, 'I was just asking Peter how he came to be a Christian.'

I didn't know what to say; fear overtook me. 'Don't let him ask me the same thing,' I thought, 'I have nothing to say.' Once again, to my utter amazement, I found myself setting down the tray on the hearth and then sitting down in the nearby armchair. We just sat there, the three of us, doing and saying nothing. We sat that way for what seemed like an age.

Then the most amazing thing happened. A blanket of heat descended upon me. I had no idea what this was but I felt, for the first time in six years, secure, safe, loved and held. Deep inside me a great warmth penetrated my being. I had never felt anything like this before.

The gentleman spoke once again, quietly this time, 'Does anyone know what is happening?'

No one spoke. We just sat there, knowing something awesome was occurring but having no idea or experience of such a time as this in our lives before; we just remained still, hardly daring to breathe.

He then began to speak to me directly, asking questions about myself. He asked me how I saw my life and I answered. For the first time in all those years I could talk about my feelings but this time without a tear, without the churning feeling inside me; just peace, amazing peace and a deep certainty of being held firmly.

He then began to tell me things from God about myself that no one could know; feelings, hopes and desires – I was lost for words. He asked if he could pray for me as he believed God was present by His Holy Spirit and wanted to touch my life. I had no idea what he meant and the cynical part of me, still somewhere in evidence, thought, 'What have I got to lose? He may as well'. So I shrugged my shoulders and nodded my head. He began to pray, asking the Lord Jesus to touch my life and to heal me. Waves of heat flooded my body still further; I radiated heat from top to toe.

'What gifts would you like Jesus to give you?'

'Gifts from God?' I thought, 'I don't even know what they are.' He must have sensed this as he listed the spiritual gifts – knowledge, wisdom, healings and miracles, discernment, faith, tongues and interpretation and prophecy (1 Cor 12:7-11). I thought a moment, I didn't really have a clue what most of them meant but had always wondered about tongues and healing sounded amazing, so that's what I asked for. He asked God to give them to me and then he stopped praying.

In an instant I knew I was healed. I stood up and went over to Peter and we stood together in the middle of the room, holding each other. I was glowing all over and I whispered,

'I've got my life back; I've got my life back.'

I knew that my mind and emotions were free; free from the darkness that had ruled them for so many years; free from the tearing pain and relentless thoughts of despair and destruction. And my body – the pain had gone; the joints were free of pain! I felt like a child again, like running and jumping; it was all so amazing. But more than anything I was experiencing the love of God, a love that had such a depth it was and still is impossible to put into words. I was 'in love' with Jesus, born-again again, as I have since put it. The power of God had come upon me, saturated me in His presence and His anointing had indeed, as the Word tells us (Isaiah 10:27 KJV), destroyed the yoke of bondage that had ruled over my life.

My request was met. I did go to church in the new year

and I was greeted with enthusiasm, not, I felt, because I was Peter's wife, coming to church for the first time, but as if I was the latest project, the one who must be in need of prayer. They knew nothing, of course, of what had happened over the past thirty-six hours.

I was so full of peace and joy I didn't care what anyone thought. I know my perceived attitude of those around me not to be true, as they were and still are a people who love the Lord and show great love for others. But having been an 'outsider' for so many years and now part of the family, as it were, I could see from both sides. It felt so good to be back, worshipping the Lord, hearing the Word and then, a new experience for me having come through rather traditional church life, it was suggested that we broke into small groups for prayer. My group of around six people gathered together and all looked at me.

'How can we pray for you? What needs do you have, Kate?'

I wanted to laugh and run around the hall. Needs? I had none; Jesus had met them all but I couldn't explain and so I just said that I had none. Of course, I knew they didn't believe me; here I was, the missing wife, poor Peter, she was in denial too!

The service ended and a lady stayed behind sitting with me and making conversation. She told me she had a neck collar on for her arthritis and before I knew it, I was asking if I could pray for her. She told me she had tried many medications for the pain and stiffness. The severity of her condition only seemed to excite something in me even more. I prayed for Jesus to heal her and to my utter amazement she told me all her pain had gone, she was healed. I knew nothing about healing, I only knew what had happened to me, but for that to happen to someone else too and because I had simply asked Jesus to do it . . . what was this all about?

Whilst this was occurring my poor husband, still in shock over the past days events and trying to grapple with what it all meant for us, was watching and panicking within himself. He saw this lady in deep conversation with me, possibly praying for me and, recalling the past years of my reaction to anyone even trying to speak to me, thought that I would never return to church again. How startled he was when I excitedly told him on the way home that I had prayed for this lady and God had healed her.

During the coming weeks, I fell deeply in love with Jesus in a way I had never experienced before. So much so that, for the first time ever, I genuinely prayed to Jesus words I would never have imagined I could say: 'If I never receive my sight back, it doesn't matter any more. You are first in my life now and all I need.'

At that moment I believe a sigh was heard in heaven. At last, Jesus Christ was Lord of my life, my 'first' love. This is God's desire for all of us, not forced by Him but that we should have a personal desire to place Him first in our lives, to surrender all to Him because of our great love for Him and all He sacrificed for us by dying on the cross. We can't cultivate this desire in ourselves, it is put there as a gift from God as we simply ask Him to come into our lives.

Within a few weeks of this prayer I realised that my sight was being restored to me. At first just little things caught my attention; things around me were becoming 'lit up'. Details began to appear. As I washed up the pots one morning I looked down and with great excitement could see my fingers in the bubbles of the washing up water. When having a cup of tea, I noticed a series of dots on the back of a Rich Tea biscuit and I clearly recall stopping in my tracks whilst crossing the garden with a handful of washing, heading for the washing line, as in astonishment I could see my feet walking.

These were amazing days as my eyesight slowly began to improve. One evening I excitedly called the family to the bathroom; I had been taking something out of the bathroom cabinet and suddenly noticed, in the mirrored cabinet doors, a reflection of the hand basin, toilet and bath. I stood in awe, looking first in the mirror and then at the bathroom and then back again, pointing excitedly.

'Look,' I cried. 'They're in the opposite order in the mirror, it's so clever, look girls.'

They were greatly amused by this as there seemed nothing too amazing in a reflection but to me, I hadn't remembered that such things existed. My sight continued to improve to being partially sighted over a period of about six weeks. I clearly recall Victoria racing upstairs one Sunday after church when the power of God touched me once more and there was a surge of improvement. She dashed back into the front room clutching her favourite book.

'Mummy, Mummy, you can read to me now.' For the first time I sat with my lovely little girls and read them a story – *Spot Goes on Holiday*.

My greatest joy was to see my husband and two beautiful daughters for the first time. Peter was so apprehensive. 'What if you don't like me?' he nervously suggested but he need have no fears, I decided to keep him on! I spent many wonderful hours just gazing at the girls, taking in their pretty faces much to their embarrassment, but as I explained to them all, I had much lost time to make up for.

Meal times were amusing to me as we sat together around the kitchen table, the waft of fish fingers, waffles and baked beans permeating the air as Amy Grant's 'Songs from the Loft', a favourite cassette, played in the background. We were enjoying the usual end of day family banter. Stories from the school day, tales about school

'. . . my lovely little girls . . .'

friends and the dramatic replays of various confrontations between teacher and pupils. As the girls chattered away I noticed Victoria's little hand reaching across the table for yet more tomato sauce.

'Victoria!' I exclaimed, 'I think you've had sufficient sauce, don't you?' She jumped visibly. Caught out, totally unused to being observed by me, she blushed beautifully and giggled. We all had some adjusting to do.

We had many amusing moments too, as in my enthusiasm to be independent, we went off to the local supermarket. I wielded the trolley and dashed ahead. The colours on the tins and packets were just wonderful as I peered around collecting beans, cereal, washing powder and various other colourful items. As we approached the final straight and the crisps aisle, I excitedly announced to Peter, 'There's no need to bother about getting the crisps, I have them.'

As I said this, I snatched the bag of crisps he was holding in his hand, tossing it nonchalantly back onto the shelf. As I proudly turned towards the checkout, Rebecca tapped me on the shoulder.

'That wasn't Daddy!' she whispered. I was horrified and turned back to see a man standing in front of the shelf, his empty hand still in the air. I apologised profusely, stumbling over my words, my face now a deep shade of beetroot, explaining that I was partially sighted. He remained static, silently looking ahead in utter bemusement.

As Peter and I began to read the Word together the Lord began to convict me to come into line with it, as it were. Having read the verse 'Repent and be baptised . . .' (Acts 2:38), I knew that this was a command from God, not an option. It was an outward declaration of what had taken place in my life. I knew I had to do this, but how? I was really frightened. I'd never seen a baptism, only heard them and the picture I had in my mind totally terrified me, but I felt too foolish to ask. However, my fear was no excuse to push this under the carpet and the knowledge of what I must do hounded me. As almost every other sermon seemed to mention baptism, there seemed no escape. In despair, I asked the Lord to give me a solution.

I was reminded by God of our lifelong friends, Bill and

Eeva-Liisa. Bill is a Baptist pastor and they are a most loving and compassionate couple as well as having a great gift of bringing joy into many of life's difficult situations. We had spent many wonderful half-term holiday weeks with them and their two children, Timothy and Eleanor, whom our two girls always looked forward to meeting up with, as we'd always have much fun and laughter together. I wrote to him asking for his help. He was so excited as he spoke to me on the phone. We arranged to go and stay for a week in Leigh-on-Sea, their home at this time, where Bill would baptise me during the Sunday evening service. I didn't want to be tipped backwards under the water, as that was too much for me to cope with and so we agreed that I would just bend my knees and go forwards into the water instead.

The Sunday evening came and dressed in my long blue baptismal gown, my hair tied back into a long ponytail, I gave my testimony, the story of my life so far and how Jesus had changed my life in so many ways and how I was experiencing His great love. God used it to touch lives, many in the youth group, who enthusiastically attended and sang a beautiful song for the occasion. But most especially, I recall, the Sunday school leader of around twenty years who had resisted the idea of baptism as he, like me, had been christened as a child in the Methodist church and didn't see, until that evening, why adult baptism was necessary. He immediately went to Bill after the service and asked to be baptised; how amazing is the convicting power of the Holy Spirit after all those years of man's attempted persuasion. 'Not by might, nor by power, but by my Spirit, says the LORD of hosts' (Zechariah 4:6).

The sight of us descending into the baptismal pool brought first amusement as Bill, at well over six feet, stood, water hardly above his knees and I, somewhat shorter, waded in up to my waist. He lined me up with my back

almost at the edge of the pool behind me. The congregation, of course, were expecting Bill to tip me backwards.
There were audible gasps as he held my back and prepared to baptise me – they all thought I was going to give
my head a crashing blow! I'm sure there was great relief
and amazement as I went under the water forwards but
I didn't care what anyone thought, all those months of
anxiety were gone; I felt so elated that I had done it.

The sense of delight and relief that was to come over
me during the following months when baptism was mentioned was immeasurable. I was beginning to discover that
only full obedience to God's Word can bring us total peace
of mind and great freedom. He always has a way to help us
achieve this, however difficult we may feel, it seems.

As our week's stay went on, Eeva-Liisa became increas-
ingly more concerned about me at mealtimes. As everyone else tucked into her home cooking I faced once again
my now meagre diet of Ryvita, boiled egg, banana and
ham. Anything other than these foods would give me
such intolerable pain for many hours, leaving me totally
incapacitated for days after each attack. Even during this
restricted eating, pain and upsets would hit me out of the
blue and each day was ruled by uncertainty. It was not just
frustrating to me but was of course not helping my body to
function well either.

We fell into conversation over the meal table about this.
'Will you pray for God to heal me?' I enquired of Bill.

He was somewhat taken aback, I think, by my request
but all of a sudden I knew that God was going to heal me
through his prayer. As a pastor, he arranged for back up in
the form of two lovely people from his own church and,
of course, Eeva-Liisa and Peter. We were all going to get
together the night before we left and then they would ask
God to heal me. As we were leaving for a long motorway
drive home on the Saturday and knowing the shops would

be closed by the time we arrived there, we went to the local supermarket. It was a time of great amusement for me, as being so certain of God's promised healing I began to request foods for my shopping trolley.

'Sausages, great fat ones please.'

'Bread buns – huge white ones.'

'Cakes, yummy chocolate.'

My mouth was watering at the prospect, indeed everything that was previously forbidden went into the trolley. Bill kept coming nervously back along the aisles, peering into my trolley and asking me in a pleading tone,

'Wouldn't you prefer some nice eggs or a bunch of bananas?'

'How about a lovely piece of plain fish to begin with?'

I strode confidently to the check out, Peter and the girls giggling in amusement at what was going on. We paid the bill and headed back to their home, triumphant. The excitement of the Lord had got hold of me and I couldn't wait for the evening to come.

As we gathered together that evening in their front room, it looked like a scene from the TV programme *Mastermind*. They sat me on a chair in the middle of the room, facing Bill. I was somewhat amused by this but I knew just how terribly nervous Bill was. Various folks read words of Scripture and we sang a few choruses, it was a very peaceful time. Then the moment came for Bill to pray. There was a nervous silence and then his humour came to the fore.

'I feel like the sausages of Damocles are hanging over me,' he said.

We laughed and began to relax and Bill began to pray. He simply asked God in His mercy and love to heal me. When we had finished praying he looked at me:

'Anyone for a sausage sandwich?'

I felt this was a bit too much too soon after such a long

time eating literally nothing at all but I said I would have a biscuit, not just a plain one but a custard cream and a cup of tea. Even that, I knew, would have sent me within minutes into agonies of pain.

So there I was, surrounded, as they all watched me take the first bite and then the next, until the whole delicious custard cream biscuit had gone. It was as if they watched for a volcano to erupt but I knew God had healed me. He had given me faith to believe, I didn't have it for myself in my own strength but it was a gift from him. Their church knew all about that evening's prayer time and was apparently listening eagerly for each week's Sunday morning service update on my eating habits.

'She's had sausages!'

'She's had fish and chips!'

'She's had a bar of chocolate!'

'All things are possible for one who believes' (Mark 9:23). When our lives are touched by God and we are open to His leading and agree with His will, many doors begin to open for us and His blessings become evident in our lives. He can fulfil His promises to us: 'I will restore to you the years that the swarming locust has eaten' (Joel 2:25).

We soon found ourselves moving house once again, this time into a bungalow only a few roads away, but in a most peaceful setting. We spent the morning of the 'move' day cleaning the house in readiness for the new occupants. My mum, who had come to help us, asked Peter to pull out the kitchen fridge in order to clean behind it, as it was tucked under the work surface. As she crouched down, dustpan and brush in hand, she gave a horrified exclamation.

'Kate, what on earth are all these old cornflakes doing down here?'

Peter and I looked across the kitchen at each other and shared a secret smile.

'I've no idea,' I replied, 'what a disgraceful housewife I am.'

I held out my hand to Peter and for a brief moment we held hands, sharing the memory of the cornflakes incident. It appeared that handfuls of them had fallen unnoticed down the back of the work surface. He bent and kissed me lightly on the cheek.

'Thank you, Jesus,' he whispered.

I smiled up at him. 'I love you.' I was so grateful to God for all He had done in our lives.

Those years of anguish, further aggravated by the local traffic, were gone and in their place not just peace but the wonderful additional blessing of a garden pond with a waterfall. I was to spend many hours sitting on the wall by the water, reading God's Word and receiving from Him. 'The lines have fallen for me in pleasant places; indeed I have a beautiful inheritance' (Psalm 16:6).

SIX

Signs and Wonders

After the miracle I had received from God and the refreshing presence of His Holy Spirit we were both now experiencing, we began to talk and pray and read God's Word together daily, trying to find out what this was all about. Was it a one off? How long would this amazing feeling, this 'presence of the Lord' stay with me? We knew absolutely nothing – only what we could read in the Gospels and the Acts of the Apostles. It began to seem to us that this was supposed to be part of 'normal' Christian life but why hadn't we heard about it before? We invited the lovely godly man who had prayed for me back to our home. Before he answered any of our questions he told us that the day God had healed me in our home, he had prayed to the Lord as he wanted to help me but wanted to do it all God's way.

He had said to Jesus, 'If I have the opportunity to see Kate tonight and she asks me to stay for a cup of tea, then I'll know that you want me to pray for her.'

How amazed we were and how much more amazing is our Lord Jesus who is truly able to do even what seems to be the impossible. He went on to explain, through the Word, what God's plan and desire for the church really was. Isaiah 61 had a profound effect on us both. We asked him how we could find out more about living as a New Testament Christian, just as the disciples in Acts did.

Some weeks later we found ourselves driving towards Lancaster, to Ellel Grange, a Christian centre which apparently taught about this life in Christ from the Word of God. We had no idea what to expect but as we drew near to the final exit of the motorway, we began to feel quite nervous. We knew nothing about such things, what if everyone else there was really learned? Slightly anxiously, we removed our suitcases from the car and headed to the main door of what was a beautiful and extremely large country house. The atmosphere inside was more than just welcoming; there was a real sense of the presence of God, something we had never experienced in such a way before. We booked in and went up to our bedroom where we read through the notes for the weekend, outlining the programme of meetings and meals.

'Wonder what "ministry night" means?' Peter commented as he read the timetable to me.

'No idea. . . .'

The Bible teaching began that first night and we sat right on the front row so I could feel fully part of the meeting and to be near to the worship group and see the outline of the person who was teaching. As the teaching began I sat transfixed as I listened to what he was saying. He taught from the Word, the Bible, which I had both read and listened to so many times over past years, but this, this was something quite different. It came alive to me, hitting the very centre of my being it seemed. I know now that this is what the Bible means by revelation, the Word of God illuminated, brought alive by the Holy Spirit. I soaked it up like a sponge; could this really be the same book? I was so excited.

The following day, the teaching sessions continued and the worship before each teaching time was awesome, so simple but the presence of the Lord was tangible. I cried but did not know why. I felt a deep love inside me welling up towards Jesus; what was this?

Then came 'ministry night'. Still knowing nothing at all about its possible meaning, we sat in our usual places on the front row, eager to hear more from the Word. After the teaching the Holy Spirit was invited to come and minister to us. It was such a quiet and gentle request and did not prepare me at all for what was to come. There were approximately one hundred people on the course and probably another thirty on the prayer team, trained to get alongside those on the course and to pray with them if they asked for help. However, God just began to touch lives without any help from anyone. Some began to cry, some to sob and sound quite distraught; the volume of noise began to rise and I began to feel extremely anxious. Peter and I sat there, not daring to move, not daring to turn around. What was this?

After about half an hour I began to feel quite ill. I thought it was fear knotting me up inside and I asked Peter if we could leave. We stood to go but by now the aisles were full of those on the ministry team, bringing love and comfort and boxes of handkerchiefs to people. As we stood there I held tightly onto Peter's arm.

'Can you find someone to pray with me?' I murmured urgently. I felt so awful I thought a bit of help might aid the speed at which I could leave. Peter looked around the crowded room as I clung onto him trying to quell the rising feeling of panic.

'I think there's a couple right at the back who are free . . .' We threaded our way through the meeting hall and requested some help. I sat down and this couple began to talk to me, I've no idea what they asked me or what they began to pray but as they spoke out the name of Jesus, so softly over me, the power of God hit me. No blanket of warmth this time as in my front room at home – something that must have mirrored thousands of volts of electricity shot through me from top to toe. I was riveted to the spot, my whole body felt charged. They prayed on; I was unable to move but one thing I knew deep down inside: this was safe and my God had me in His powerful arms and would not let any harm come to me. For probably over an hour they prayed for me, led by the Holy Spirit and eventually the overwhelming power began to subside to leave me with the most wonderful sense of well being, a radiance I had never experienced before. From the inside out it welled up in me, I felt as if I must have shone out in the dark. I stood to my feet and felt as if I had shed a few stones in weight; my youth was renewed like never before (see Isaiah 40:30-31).

Once again, my wonderful husband looked at me in amazement. We thanked the couple, words seemed so inadequate, and made our way up the carpeted staircase to bed. I was far too excited to sleep at first but then a deep sleep overcame me. I awoke just after six and the vitality within me was tremendous. I woke poor Peter and begged him to get up and come for a swim.

'A swim?' he said, 'A swim at this time in the morning! Are you mad?'

Off we went; I felt as if I could run a marathon, the new life flowing through me was just astonishing. God had delivered me from yet more of the heavy things the past had brought into my life – the loss of my sight, the fear and sense of abandonment, humiliation and suffering. I felt set free, just as the Word says, 'So if the Son sets you free, you will be free indeed' (John 8:36).

With this new found freedom came a deep longing and desire to put my life right, even though I hadn't actually thought that there was anything wrong with it before. I didn't really know what that would mean specifically but I had such a desire in me to be the pure bride that the Word speaks about (2 Corinthians 11:2), whatever it cost. My love for Him was so overwhelming. I had done nothing to create this within me; it was the Lord Himself who had caused this transformation to happen. This is His desire, that we would love Him with all our heart, all our mind, all our soul and all our strength (Mark 12:33).

We returned home and I can only say that I floated through the following weeks in the presence of the Lord. He never left me for a moment. I would sit and just know His presence with me; we would talk together, rest together and just 'be' ('Be still and know that I am God' Psalm 46:10). I glowed for weeks, too, and my lovely little girls would just come and stand and look at me and their daddy would explain, 'She's fine, just enjoying Jesus.'

They told me I looked 'sparkly' and I guess that was it. Cleansed by the power of God, sparkly clean. We had some amazing experiences as a family during those weeks, as the presence of God filled our home.

One evening in particular after we had put the girls to bed, we were sitting, with our new thirst for the Word, reading the Bible and praying together. All of a sudden we were aware of the presence of the Lord and a beautiful perfume began to fill the room. It was so unusual, a mixture of perfume and burning wood, though that description falls far short as we had never experienced this aroma before. We must have looked rather strange going around the room sniffing the air. In awe we whispered to each other,

'What is it?'

'It's over here!' Then revelation came once more; we realised that it was the fragrance of the Lord, just as Lucy had experienced it in our housegroup many years before. He indeed was with us. We ran upstairs and woke the girls.

'Jesus is here, girls, come on!' Excitedly, we crept downstairs and quietly entered the room. The girls sniffed the air and they could smell the aroma, too.

'He's over here!' they exclaimed in excitement. We stood together in a group hug, where the perfume was at its greatest and prayed to our Jesus. It was a beautiful time and the presence and power of God stayed with us all.

The girls rushed into our bedroom the next morning, jumping onto our bed.

'I feel all springy!' exclaimed Victoria. There was something different about them both, a new energy even for children.

Over the coming months we were to have the great joy of seeing Rebecca baptised and, at the age of six, on Peter's fortieth birthday, Victoria disappeared upstairs for a short while, only to return excitedly.

'I've just asked Jesus into my life,' she beamed.

What a birthday present! We all hugged each other as we celebrated this exciting news. This Jesus was real. He affects every part of us, body, soul and spirit.

We began to have people from our home church call us to ask if they could come to our home as they had various needs, mostly, at first, physical ailments. The very first time this occurred we were very anxious, as we had nothing to offer of ourselves, which is just as God would have it. What should we do? What should we pray? Human weakness arose and doubts filled our minds. What if nothing happens? What if we can't help? As our first visitor, a good friend, was due to arrive in just under one hour, we thought we had better ask the Lord what He suggested. To my astonishment, as we prayed I saw in front of my eyes, for the very first time, words. It was a Scripture verse, just the Bible reference (Luke 5:12). We looked it up and we read about a man being healed of a 'dreaded skin disease'. What did this mean? We wanted some specific instructions; how could this help us?

Then, before we had time to think any further, our friend rang the doorbell and we had invited him in. He was rather nervous and somewhat embarrassed. We talked 'around the houses' until in desperation I asked, 'How can we help you?' He shyly told us that he had problems with the skin on his face. He was constantly struggling, and had been for years, with a severe rash, like cold sores around his mouth, causing him much embarrassment. Excitement began to rise within me, I was astonished – the Scripture, the skin disease. I picked up the open Bible beside me and held it out to him.

'Look what Jesus told us to look at just before you came.'

He took the Bible and read the passage. He was just as amazed as we were, but God had increased our faith in that very moment. We prayed, asking Him, according to His Word, to bring healing. How excited we were when a short while later we had a phone call to tell us that all the skin problems had gone completely. Years later, as we continued in our friendship, he was still enjoying his healing.

Of course, through this incident of God's leading and power being shown, our faith, probably even smaller than a mustard seed at first, began to grow. We dared to believe that the whole of God's Word was as true and certain today as it obviously was in the days of Jesus and His disciples: 'Jesus Christ is the same yesterday and today and forever' (Hebrews 13:8). We began to pray that God would equip us further, teach us more and more from His Word and open doors of opportunity to touch lives through His power and because of His love and mercy. As God began to answer our prayers, our girls also began to see lives amazingly changed and restored. They began to know for themselves that Jesus was a miracle-working Saviour and that, if we prayed to Him, believing, He would answer. Not always as we expected or perhaps wanted, not always as instantly as we would prefer, but always in time – His perfect time and the very best for us.

Rebecca still had problems with her left knee as a result of her hip surgery as a young child. Now, at the age of twelve, she was still visiting the General Hospital to see her surgeon for regular check-ups. Having been X-rayed once again, he told us that she needed surgery on her knee. It would often dislocate without warning, causing extreme pain and swelling for many days. She was unable to participate in sport or to run, jump or climb. Rebecca was very frightened at the prospect of going into hospital and we all knew that Jesus could heal her and so, as a family, we began to pray, asking Him to do so.

During a holiday week in North Yorkshire we decided to visit Hollybush Christian Fellowship, held in a converted barn on a farm. They held evening meetings as well as Sunday services. We had never had the opportunity to go there until now. This was a church that believed that God's will is to heal. We went to an evening meeting and after the worship time and the preaching of the Word they announced that if anyone needed healing they could come out to the front.

Peter took Rebecca out whilst I stayed with Victoria. A lady approached them and asked what the problem was. Peter explained about her knee. Amazingly, the lady had just that week seen a programme about that very problem and was able to pray with knowledge for Rebecca's knee to be healed. They thanked her and came back to join us as the service continued.

Rebecca turned to me and said, 'Come on Mummy, it's your turn now, Jesus can finish healing your eyes.'

I must admit I was not eager at that time as I knew what upset it caused the girls when that particular prayer was not answered immediately. However, Rebecca was insistent and so I went out with her and two ladies began to pray for me. I stood there, eyes shut, asking God to stop them as I just knew that this was not the time. Then to my great upset I felt Rebecca's hand in mine begin to shake.

'Oh no,' I thought, 'she's crying. Now look what's happened.' I opened my eyes and turned to the two ladies.

'Would you mind if we stopped?' I said tentatively. 'I think my daughter is getting upset.'

To my astonishment, as we made our way back to our seats, I realised that she was not crying at all, just shaking under the power of God. He had poured out His Spirit upon her, filling her to overflowing. She sat down and we began to pray for her, Victoria joining in, too. She peered at her sister, the bunches in her hair swinging against my knees.

'What's the matter with Rebecca, Mummy?' She reached out her hand and touched her sister's knee. 'She's shaking, just like a telegraph wire with birds sitting on it, dithering, like in a comic.'

She was right. Just then with a shriek of delight Rebecca noticed that her usually swollen podgy knee had shrunk, just like a deflating balloon, and now she had a knobbly knee just like the other one! Peter went in great excitement, threading his way through the chattering congregation, to tell the church pastor, Jim Wilkinson, just what had happened. He brought her out to the front.

'Run around the hall, go on, as fast as you can.' he said. She did. This was a first in her life, running freely, on the flat and up the steps. Wow, we were so amazed and the room buzzed with excited voices as they watched her progress and the huge smile on her face. She was so full of God's Spirit we practically carried her to the car. 'Some, however, made fun of them and said, "They have had too much wine"' (Acts 2:13 NIV).

Some weeks later we returned to the specialist and he took another X-ray of her knee.

'Hmm,' he mused. 'It would appear that it is perfect. Perhaps we'll keep you on the list for surgery just in case. . . .' I smiled as he paused and looked across at me, 'On the other hand, I've just seen your mummy's face and we'll take you off the list straight away.' He continued, 'If God were to do this all the time, I would be out of a job!'

Later, Victoria was to encounter the same healing power of God as she fell badly whilst roller skating. In great pain, we were sent to the local cottage hospital on a sleepy Sunday afternoon. The on-call doctor took one look at it and sent us on our way to the main hospital as he decided it was a bad fracture or possibly a break. As we sat in casualty, we laid our hands on Victoria's arm.

We prayed, 'Just as you healed Becki's knee, Jesus, and because you love them both just the same, please heal Victoria.'

Off she went for her X-ray and returned with a rather bemused doctor.

'It seems the arm is fine, just bruised. She can go home!'

He might have been surprised at the outcome but we weren't. We understood. Jesus had once again reached out with His hand of healing and touched one of His children.

We saw this once again some years later in Victoria's life as, when pouring out hot water one tea time, the lid of the boiling kettle fell off and scalding water flowed over the whole of her left hand. Her screams were dreadful as I held her hand under cold water and we rang the surgery to say we needed to bring her in straight away. We began to pray for God to touch her skin and bring complete healing. As the nurse at the surgery applied cream and strapping to her hand, she exclaimed in a most discouraging tone,

'This is a severe burn, it will take a time to recover and you'll always have some scarring.'

Victoria cried and I kept my arm tight around her.

'It's going to be all right, Jesus will sort it out,' I whispered in her ear.

We went home, believing in our wonderful Jesus and thanking Him in faith for what He was going to do. Three days later we returned to the nurse so that the dressing could be changed. Her astonished voice thrilled us.

'My goodness, it's all but gone!' The dressing removed, there was only a slightly pink skin and the remnants of a few partial blisters. Within a short while the skin was totally renewed and Victoria could use her hand perfectly once again. What a Mighty God we serve.

We began to realise through reading His Word that the Scripture, 'My grace is sufficient for you, for my power is made perfect in weakness' (2 Corinthians 12:9), was indeed true. As we give ourselves, just as we are, even though we may feel we have nothing to offer Him, He is waiting to take us and use us for His glory and to bring rich blessings into the lives of His creation. We realised that total obedience was the key; total submission to Him was crucial in order for His power to flow through us. This was our choice to make, of course. He loves us unconditionally and will never force us to do anything; it is our own choice, but, as with anyone we truly love, there comes the desire to please.

This would enable those with great needs to be brought to a new level of knowing His love and freedom. God began to show us where we needed to 'clean up' our lives in order to walk a more godly and holy life. We asked the Holy Spirit to show us anything that was hindering our walk with Him, anything with content that was not a good influence on our lives. He began to remind us of books, old LPs, cassettes and other personal items, mostly in the loft or tucked away in cupboards or on bookshelves. They hadn't been looked at or listened to for years, but nevertheless they were in our home and so they had to go.

It was, of course, our choice as God will never make

any of us do anything against our will, but we so desired to be a pure bride for Him, because of our love for Him, that we were willing to get rid of anything He showed us. He began to point out television programmes, both serious and humorous, not that God is lacking in a sense of humour; He delights in us living in great joy. Some of these programmes, however, contained language and scenes which were not honouring to His name.

I recall at this time a particular programme that was shown on a Sunday evening. We enjoyed it but the content was somewhat dubious. However, in spite of the fact we were just learning how to be led by the Holy Spirit, we recorded it on the video player so we wouldn't miss it whilst out at church. When we returned home we made a cup of tea and sat down to watch it. Having rewound the tape, we pressed play and up on the screen came a programme about the broad and the narrow way (Matthew 7:13-14)! It was a half hour programme talking about both those different paths, what we might expect to encounter on these differing paths and the effect it would have on our lives. You can imagine how shocked we were; where was our programme, and more to the point, what was God trying to say? We were glued to the programme, knowing deep down inside that He was calling us to walk the narrow way with Him and rid ourselves even more of those things He would show us, if we were willing.

When the programme finished, we just looked at each other in awe of God's power to intervene in any part of our lives, even technology. Just a mistake with the video settings, I hear you thinking. We thought that, too. After we had prayed together, we rewound the tape, thinking that if we went through the programme again God could speak to us more, as we were over the initial shock of finding it there. However, to confirm to us that it was indeed His supernatural intervention, another shock awaited us.

There on the screen was our planned sitcom programme, opening credits and music, the whole thing. You might imagine our reaction – we fast forwarded the tape, rewound it, pressed play, then repeated the process again and again in an attempt to find 'The Broad and the Narrow Way' but it was not to be found anywhere, not even in the *Radio Times*! Only our comedy programme, as if God was saying, 'Now what are you going to do?' We switched off the television. How awesome is our God; He sees and knows everything, there is nothing impossible for Him. He will find a way of coming into our lives in order that we might receive the best for us; nothing is a barrier to Him.

Some time later I felt that God was asking me to give up a particular drama programme, again because of the content. It was a weekly drama, following many lives of different families and situations and relationships. There was some violence regularly shown in that particular series and I knew He didn't want my mind to be filled with such things: 'Finally, brothers, whatever is true . . . honourable . . . just . . . pure . . . lovely . . . commendable . . . if there is anything worthy of praise, think about these things' (Philippians 4:8). But I loved my weekly programme. I wrestled for some weeks with this until I couldn't stand it any longer. I made the decision to respond to the Holy Spirit's prompting and the following week turned off the television at the appointed hour.

At once, the television seemed to become this huge object in the corner of the room, beckoning me to watch it. It took many weeks for me to overcome this what I can only believe was an unknown addiction to this programme, but at last the desire and need to watch it faded away. At the times of struggling with whether to switch it on or not, I found my only source of help was to leave the room and go to the Word of God, where He would give me something to encourage me in my walk with Him. He taught me that nothing was too small or seemingly ridiculous to Him, He is interested in all areas of our lives and wants to hear about and help with them all, if we come to Him and ask: 'You do not have, because you do not ask' (James 4:2).

We returned to Ellel Grange every couple of months to be fed with the Word of God and to worship in His presence. Each visit, God would touch a different area of our life that needed His light to infiltrate, expose and bring us into freedom and peace. We soon realised that we needed to walk in forgiveness, forgiveness of those who had hurt us in the past and towards whom we still carried deep hurts or bitterness. Forgiveness of groups of people – hospitals, doctors and nurses, churches and some of their members, schools and their teachers and pupils, work places and their workers and even, perhaps, some of our family members and friends, both past and present.

At first the list was immense as we asked the Holy Spirit to show us who we needed to forgive. Some names were obvious; others took us by surprise but we came to realise that He was right – we held hurts and grudges, we were offended and resentful. Most of these feelings and emotions had been hidden, often in order to go on and cope with the future, but they had robbed us in the past and some ruled us in the present, stopping us in some cases from coming into the fullness of what God had for us. Some of those we had forgiven in obedience to the Word had caused us great emotional and mental damage. The unforgiveness we had held had also affected our physical being too.

It was not easy to speak out words of forgiveness. We came to realise that we could do this only as an act of our will, setting aside our emotions and walking in obedience. We found our encouragement in God's promise, which was that as we forgave, He would forgive us and set us free and heal our broken hearts. Indeed, as we continued to forgive the same people, sometimes over a period of weeks or months, over and over again as thoughts and hurts from the past came to us, He did amazingly do just that. The bitterness and resentment left us, and in its place came a great peace. God used one particular relationship to take us further on in our experience of understanding His unconditional love for all.

We had come into conflict with a Christian brother. Our church was due to select a new team of deacons. Members of the congregation suggested possible candidates and after a number of weeks seeking the Lord in prayer would decide who they felt were right for the position. The Sunday this was announced in church I was approached by two people to stand for one of the places. As Peter and I climbed into the car to go home after the service, the girls chattering away in the back seat, it appeared that Peter, too, had been approached. This left us in a quandary as, to keep a fair balance of opinion, husbands and wives could not take up office at the same time. So, one of us had to stand down before the decisions were made. Peter encouraged me to go ahead but I wasn't sure. He was more mature in his faith, steadfast, gentle and, I felt, full of wisdom and a steady influence. I needed time to seek God.

'What do you want me to do, Jesus?' I prayed over and over again as the weeks moved on. Two days before the church made their decision I had a vivid dream and as I awoke I knew that I had to withdraw my name.

We had a phone call that evening from a leader in our church asking if he could come round to see us the following evening. We had no idea what it was about but gladly said yes. He came with his wife and it became apparent very quickly that he had something to say. He knew nothing of my decision but was obviously unhappy at the prospect of me, a woman, standing instead of Peter. He quickly moved the conversation onto the subject of women in the church. He became very verbally aggressive and directed some extremely hurtful remarks at me; Peter was unable to stop his tirade. His words not only shocked me as they became quite personal but deeply wounded me too. The Lord held me together emotionally until he had left, for which I was extremely grateful, but then I fell apart. How could anyone speak to a fellow believer and a younger woman in that way, cutting me down and trampling my feelings and dignity underfoot?

Throughout the following weeks, that incident kept coming into my mind. Whenever we were in the same room at church I felt great resentment and anger towards this man and the desire welled up within me to speak out what I felt about him. I longed to tell others as he chatted and laughed with them just what, in my opinion, he was really like. But the opportunity never arose to let it all out. At the same time, I began to read in the Word more about forgiveness, that the Lord Jesus needed us to walk in forgiveness in order that He might forgive us: 'And forgive us our debts, as we also have forgiven our debtors' (Matthew 6:12). More than that, the passage goes on to say, in verse 15, that 'if you do not forgive others their trespasses, neither will your Father forgive your trespasses.'

What was I to do? It seemed so unfair, after all, he had done the hurting, surely it was he that should be apologising for his rude and damaging behaviour. He was an older man in leadership and I was a young woman. However, God tells us in His Word that He is no respecter of persons, that we are all equal in His sight, 'for God shows no partiality' (Romans 2:11). Each of us is accountable to Him for our own walk – no excuses. Anyway, the only person who was being harmed was me; he was oblivious to all my pain. I was holding myself into suffering by not letting go of my grudge against him and running the risk of becoming even more bitter and resentful.

I began to realise that I had to forgive this gentleman

and go on forgiving him until all the bitter thoughts left my mind. I didn't want to forgive him; it felt as if I would be letting him off the hook, as it were. I learned through the Word, though, that it is for God to judge and deal with each individual, we are only responsible for our own walk of obedience. So, purely obeying the Lord's command, I began to speak out forgiveness towards this man.

'This is so hard, Jesus, he's hurt me so much. I can only say the words at present because I know you want me to. I'm trusting you, Lord.' My mind was fighting these words for many weeks but I kept on; every time I thought about him I spoke forgiveness and blessing.

Within a few months I discovered that, sadly, this man had recently been diagnosed with terminal cancer. It was a sudden diagnosis and the church was asked to pray. I joined with them and to my astonishment God began to give me such an overwhelming love for this man and a deep compassion for him. I spoke to his wife and Peter and I went to his home to visit. I entered the house with some trepidation, not knowing how I might be received. We walked into their sitting room and I went across and held out my hand to Philip.

'Thank you for coming,' he said.

'We wanted to,' I replied.

I meant it. We prayed together and God gave us a real compassion for him and restored our relationship. Some little time later he was admitted into hospital. We visited once again and prayed together. My heart was full of love for this man as I held his hand, which by now was so weak, asking God to pour out His love and peace upon him. Sadly, he died some weeks later and I had lost a dear friend.

I remember crying at his funeral and standing in awe of what God had been able to do in my heart and mind with this one incident. I realised that He needed me to go on walking in forgiveness daily, being quick to forgive those who might hurt me intentionally or even unintentionally, it made no difference to the Lord. This was a foundational part of my walk and one which would keep my mind and heart in great peace in the coming years as I realised, too, that the only one who suffers through holding unforgiveness is ourselves, as it eats away at us.

Our prayers for God to open doors of opportunity to walk in our new revelation of God's healing and delivering power began to be answered. We were able to bring God's love and Word into broken marriages and see Him restore them. This was the cause of much celebration and joy in our home as we saw couples arrive for a weekend stay in great distress, bitterness and anger so evident. They would leave a few days later holding hands, looking as if they were newly weds about to leave on honeymoon. One couple was returning to their three children full of the Lord's joy, as they had previously decided that they would have to break up the family, but God had stepped in as they humbled themselves before Him.

One Sunday morning we were approached by a lady after the morning service. 'What is it about you?' she asked. 'I can see something special in your family; whatever it is, I want it.'

We told her about Jesus and she immediately chose to invite Him into her own life. Two days later we visited her home, merely, we thought, to give her a Bible and some reading material. We talked for a short while and then got up to leave. She began to cry.

'I'm sorry,' she wept. 'It's just that I'm going into hospital next week. I've had breast cancer for over a year now. They've tried everything but now I have to have radical surgery. I haven't been able to hug my children for months, the pain is so great and I'm so frightened. I don't want to go through with this.'

'Can we pray for you?'

She nodded in agreement as she wiped the tears from her eyes and held onto my hand.

'Dear Lord, please give Jan your deep peace, pour in your love and let her know that you are with her.'

She continued to cry and then I heard the Holy Spirit speaking to me – 'Pray for her healing, she needs more than My peace.'

I was horrified. I mumbled to Peter, hardly daring to suggest such a thing. What if nothing happened, what if we raised her hopes and they were dashed? This was a major illness, far too huge to contemplate. But in obedience, Peter took out the small bottle of olive oil we carried with us and explained from the Bible that we would like to anoint her and pray for God to heal her. We were all stepping into the unknown together but she had no knowledge of this, she only believed what we told her from the Bible, that the sick people got well.

This healing was not our responsibility; all we had to do was be obedient to His prompting. We began to pray for God to heal her, anointing her forehead as we did so according to the Word (James 5:14). Peter took authority over the pain in Jesus' name and told it to go. It did! Jan was astonished. 'The pain, it's all gone!' she exclaimed. We were all so excited. Peter and I were full of joy and faith.

We left, assuring her we would keep praying. That night we had a phone call from a very excited lady; she told us that she was burning with heat, so much so that her husband could warm his hands on her from at least a foot away! I was amazed and we said we would go back and see her the following day.

When we got there she asked us, 'Is that oil supposed to do something?'

'Why?' I asked. She then told us that hidden under her fringe was a tumour, unseen by Peter when he anointed her with oil. Now it had completely disappeared! It transpired that she also had two more tumours in her breast the size of boiled eggs (she put my hand on one) and one under her arm. We prayed again that God would remove them and left full of excitement and faith. A few days later the tumours in her breast had gone, in fact there were holes where the tumours had been, which, after more prayer, God slowly refilled with brand new good tissue. The tumour under her arm shrank to the size of a pea; she felt this was a reminder from the Lord of the amazing thing He had done.

She returned to her consultant at a local cancer unit where they had been monitoring the size of the tumours. He was able to confirm that this was indeed only explained by the word 'miracle'. They had closely examined all her notes and progress charts. The impossible had happened.

Needless to say, her husband became a Christian. As he said to us, 'How could I do any other?' Almost fifteen years on, this lady has a science degree, something she had always hoped to do in her life, and is working in a local university laboratory.

On another occasion I was in conversation after church one morning with a lady who was struggling with the effects of a brain tumour; she had very poor mobility and speech because of this. As we chatted, toddlers running between us, cups of tea rattling in saucers and the shouts of the teenagers playing football outside filled the hall. She told a group of us that she was going to have an operation to remove the tumour the following month. She had been told to learn sign language and to have her telephone adapted for the use of the deaf. Apparently, her surgery would hopefully deal with the tumour, saving her life, but as a result she would lose her hearing.

As a number of friends stood around listening, I looked straight at her and said, 'Don't have your phones changed; you're not going to go deaf.'

I was shocked. She just looked at me as if I was mad, as

did those standing around, who all fell silent. I had said it now, there was no going back, and so, with blushing cheeks, I asked her if she would like to come round to our home that week. She did and we had a wonderful time together. Towards the end of the morning, though, she became distressed and asked me to switch off the music on the cassette player.

'What if I can never hear music again?' she sobbed.

She was so afraid she wouldn't be able to hear these things anymore after her operation. We wept together as I stood, my hands over her ears, asking Jesus to heal her. She grabbed hold of my hand.

'I can't bear the thought of not hearing my husband's voice ever again.'

'Jesus,' I prayed, silently, 'You can do it, Lord, I know you can.'

A few weeks later she was admitted into hospital for her major surgery. I had prayed throughout the previous weeks and on that day most particularly, standing in faith and thanking God for what He was about to do so that He might have all the glory and praise. Of course, from time to time small doubts would hit my mind as the enemy whispered mocking words to me.

'What have you done? She'll never hear again and you told her not to learn sign language.'

But God had caused me to speak this promise out, surely He would fulfil what He had promised? That night Peter and I visited her in hospital. As I approached the room where she lay I must admit it was with fear and trembling that I pushed open the door and peered into a gloomily lit room.

'Hello Kate,' her smiling voice said. Instantly I knew that God had indeed kept His promise and that she could hear. She was so excited and her husband, sitting at her bedside, was so shocked that God could do such an amazing thing: 'but with God all things are possible' (Matthew 19:26).

SEVEN

Moving Forward

Both Peter and I began to have a burning desire to serve God, not just a bit here and a bit there, but to serve Him fully. He had given us such a great love and compassion for those in need of His touch in their lives. We spoke to a lovely Christian couple, Jim and Muriel, about this. They told us that we were already serving God 'full time' and that for all Christians, wherever God places us is our 'mission field'. We needed to submit to Him where we were and begin to ask Him to bring opportunities to us. We were somewhat disappointed in this response, as we had hoped they would point out to us some amazing ministry that we could move into, but at the same time we recognised in this godly couple a maturity in the Lord, a humble nature, instead of one of pride, that we needed to have. So in prayer we submitted our future to the Lord, just as the Scripture says: 'present your bodies as a living sacrifice, holy and acceptable to God' (Romans 12:1).

We sat together one evening, held hands and prayed. 'We want to follow you, Jesus. We'll go anywhere, do anything you ask us to do.'

We had no idea what a dangerous prayer that was. We only knew that we had to pray it because we loved our Jesus so much. God answers all our prayers prayed in faith, believing, and He longs to give us the desires of our hearts (Psalm 37:4).

We settled our minds to continuing with our daily lives, Peter teaching full time, me taking some part-time teaching and looking after the children and the house. We led a mid-week evening Bible study meeting in our home, a worship practice each Friday night and during the day I led a prayer and Bible study group for ladies. Our house was full of people and lots of laughter, both day and night. We were extremely contented with our life; we had much fun and games with our lovely children, who were growing into very loving, gentle and full-of-fun girls each with their own personalities. But deep within us remained the desire to do more for the Lord. We had no idea what, but a sense that 'something' was going to happen began to stir in us. We continued to seek God, praying together and reading His Word, trusting for His leading and perfect timing.

One evening as Peter went around the house switching off electrical items, locking doors and generally checking the house for the night, he was walking across the lounge when God spoke to him in an audible voice.

'Peter.'

He stopped in his tracks.

'Yes Lord?' he said, knowing it was the audible voice of Jesus Himself.

'Feed my lambs.'

That was all, but Peter knew he had met with God and been instructed by Him. Some weeks later as we continued seeking the Lord, a lady from our church came to the door. She was very excited and told me that God had given her a 'word' for me. Of course, we have to be very careful when someone comes to us with such things. The Bible teaches us that we must test everything against the Word of God (1 Thessalonians 5:21) and so I was willing to let her share it with me. She sat down and read out what God had given her. I don't recall it all, only that she kept repeating the words 'feed my sheep'. I didn't need to check that out with the Word as I knew these instructions were to be found in John 21. God was speaking, confirming to us both what He would have us do. But where, doing what and when?

Soon afterwards we heard that the local education authority required some schools to reduce their overall budget by losing a member of staff. What a terrible task for each head of school. The governors met together in Peter's school and decided that each staff member's job description should be submitted to them, without their names on, in order to make the committee's choice impersonal. This was duly done and the decision as to whom they should lose was made. There were twelve staff in Peter's junior school, ten were women, mostly on second incomes and it was felt that one of them would be chosen or perhaps offered early retirement.

However, the day of reckoning came and we had a great sense that God was in this with us. Peter left for work as usual and I got on with my housework. By the afternoon I had, unbelievably, forgotten all about it. To my surprise, the kitchen door was flung open and in walked Peter. I checked the time, three o'clock, how odd. I turned to him in jest, brandishing the potato peeler, and said,

'What's happened, have you got the sack?'

'Yes,' he replied, 'I have! It seems my areas of responsibility overlap with a number of other teachers and so I am the chosen one.'

His face lit up with laughter, he held out his arms to me and I ran into them. I remembered. We danced around the kitchen together; we were not, as you might expect, devastated at Peter losing his job, but excited because God had so unexpectedly brought him out of teaching. We were on our way forward. Of course, the staff were shocked, our family were shocked, some were outraged that such a thing had happened, but we knew that this was what we had been waiting for. The staff marvelled at Peter's joy and peace in the remaining weeks at work. We had no idea what God had in store for us but at the end of the summer term we signed on the dole. This was a totally new experience for us and without realising it we were being prepared for a time when we needed to manage our lives with a lot less available finances. What were we to do next? God had clearly brought us out of teaching but into what?

We had over the past few years been greatly involved in our local church fellowship, Peter preaching and teaching regularly, holding house groups and prayer meetings in our home, leading worship and pastoral care. Some of the deacons and members of the congregation came to us and told us that they felt that we should go into the Baptist ministry. That seemed a wonderful idea, something we would really love to do together. We began to pray and put into place the process of applying for the ministry.

Peter was given an interview in Manchester at the Baptist training college and, dressed in his suit and tie, nervously set off. It went well and the process continued. The final hurdle was for the deacons to meet together to pray and discuss our suitability and to complete a questionnaire about us. We knew they would come to their verdict that night and that the superintendent for the area would be coming straight to our home to give us the news. It was, as the deacons said, a foregone conclusion; after all, our church having had no pastor for over a year now, we had been fulfilling much of that role for some time already, it made such sense.

We sat expectantly at home until the doorbell rang. Peter showed in the gentleman; he seemed rather subdued, I thought, for someone bringing such good news. He nervously sat down and got straight to the point.

'I'm afraid to tell you that you have been turned down.'

He must have seen the shock and disbelief on our faces. I can't remember what else he said but within minutes, excusing himself and saying he thought we would like time on our own, he left. After all that build up over so many weeks, we sat looking at each other, silently contemplating what had just happened. We hugged each other and cried. We had been so sure that this was God's plan for us – what could be the matter with us?

The next day one of our good friends, also a deacon, rang to commiserate with us. I asked him why we had been turned down. He told me that there were five specific questions they needed to be able to say 'yes' to. They had been able to do that for all but the last one.

'What was the problem?' I asked in trepidation.

Apparently, it was the last question, 'Do you believe they are called to the *Baptist* ministry', that caused the problem. The stumbling block was that they couldn't say 'yes'. I was shocked.

'But why?'

'Because we know you are both called to ministry but we didn't feel you were Baptist enough!'

At that very moment something seemed to lift off me. I felt free and when I shared the conversation with Peter we found ourselves recognising that it was true. We had no particular denominational pull within us; we were just Christians, followers of the Lord Jesus, just like the disciples in the Bible. What a revelation. This was obviously something major that God needed to show us in order to prepare us for the specific call on our lives.

We had much prayer support and encouragement from friends at this time, especially within our church family, for, though He does not want us to be bound up with one particular denomination, He does want us to be fully committed to a church family. Sadly, there were also those who doubted what we were doing. They voiced their doubts to us, most unhelpfully. One lady in particular, who worked in the local Christian bookshop, would greet us each and every time we went in with the words,

'Oh dear, are you still here? Don't you know what you are doing yet?'

Her voice conveyed to us that she didn't believe what we were saying, as each time we replied, 'Not yet, we are waiting for God to show us.'

It was so hard. The devil used this each time to pour fresh doubt on what we believed God was doing in our lives. We had to fight in our minds the negative words, renewing our minds through the Word and reminding ourselves of what God had spoken to us so far ('for we walk by faith, not by sight' 2 Corinthians 5:7).

Two months had passed by now and there we were, back to square one. Now what? Some days, panic would arise in us – what if we'd got it all wrong? Perhaps Peter had just been given the sack and that was that, perhaps God wasn't in this at all! We obviously needed to do something; training would be necessary, we thought, we needed to be equipped for whatever it was God wanted us to do. We began to contact Bible colleges around the UK. Within a few weeks we had a huge stack of prospectuses, unopened. We set aside a day, drove off to the nearby North Yorkshire Moors and parked the car in a remote spot. With the pile of brochures on my knee we prayed.

'Lord, please show us which college you want us to go to; we want to get it right.' One by one we opened them, read through them, waiting for the Holy Spirit to bring a particular one to our notice. However, a few hours later we looked at each other once again – nothing, not a stirring. We were really stuck for ideas now.

Home we went, quite despondent and then, in desperation, we had a really good idea. Why not pray and simply ask God what He wanted us to do? It seems incredible that we had not specifically done this in all those months but often, as Christians, we run around after good ideas and suggestions from others instead of going directly to the throne of God and seeking Him for His perfect will and purpose for our lives. ' "For I know the plans I have for you," declares the Lord, "plans to prosper you and not to harm you, plans to give you hope and a future" ' (Jeremiah 29:11 NIV).

Some weeks later as we continued to seek the Lord for our future, telling Him once more that we would do anything He asked us to do, we heard that the Hollybush fellowship, around twenty miles from our home, was running a Bible week. We were unable to stay there ourselves but it was near enough to go for an evening meeting. So off we set and squeezed into seats in the packed converted barn. I have no idea who spoke that night as during the worship, for the first time ever, I saw a picture in front of my eyes. It was a torch, the usual battery-type torch.

'How odd,' I thought, 'what was that all about?' I tried to put it from my mind but couldn't. When we arrived home I told Peter about this. We got out our Bible concordance and looked up the word 'torch'. There were passages about Gideon and the torchbearers and those who carried torches to the garden where Jesus was betrayed but none of it seemed to make any sense. I gave it up as just a strange but unimportant happening. However, the word 'torch' kept on nagging at my mind; I would see that picture again and again as I began to pray or even when I was just hoovering or washing up. Then, after some time, a thought came into my mind.

Years earlier, Peter had offered to drive for a faith ministry called Torch Trust for the Blind. They had what were called fellowship groups all around the country where visually impaired people met once a month for Christian fellowship and to listen to a speaker and have tea together.

They needed people to drive for them on a Saturday afternoon and so, for some years, we would collect a number of
people from their homes, drop them off at the meeting and
then return for them a few hours later. The helpers, discovering that I was blind, would come out to the car quite
often and ask if I would like to come in and join them. I
always declined, as I was not at all interested in spending
Saturday afternoon with other blind people. I was young
and independent and wanted very much to stay that way.

I did visit once, though, as Peter and I belonged to a music
group. We sang and played guitars, recorders and sometimes tin whistles, being quite folky in much of our music.
We had great times and much laughter and really enjoyed
ministering in this way. Our good friend and pastor, Bill,
invited us to help him out one Saturday afternoon as he was
speaking at a Torch meeting in Middlesbrough, and so we
sang a few songs. Being the one and only blind person in the
group, not that I had really thought about that, I was greeted
with great enthusiasm and taken off to meet other blind
people and to sit with them for tea. I have to say I didn't
enjoy it, as I only wanted to be with my husband and friends
and feel part of the 'sighted community' once again.

As this seed of a thought, planted during that Bible
week, began to grow in my mind, to my horror I found
myself thinking that maybe God was asking us to work
for Torch. My heart sank; no, that couldn't possibly be
right. I was no longer blind but partially sighted, heading
towards the sighted world – surely God wouldn't send me
back to be with loads of blind people? I fought off these
thoughts for a few weeks not daring to share them with
Peter, knowing that he, too, had no thoughts of anything
in that direction.

However, I can only say I began to be plagued with the
word 'torch' and finally, very early one Monday morning,
in desperation for peace, I got up, crept downstairs in my

dressing gown and sat at the kitchen table. It was so peaceful, the sun just glinting on the window and the birdsong as a backdrop to my thinking.

I said to the Lord, 'If you want me to find out more about this Torch business then you will have to show me by Friday and if you don't, then I will totally forget about it all.'

Having issued my ultimatum to God, I felt much better and went back upstairs to wake the children and get everyone ready for the day ahead. I knew that it was not possible for Him to speak to me about something I had no connection with. I happily went on with my week, beginning to celebrate in my mind the release I was going to feel when nothing had happened by Friday.

The post arrived on Friday morning and with it a yellow plastic wallet, which I was familiar with as I received many talking newspapers, magazines and other material recorded onto cassette for visually impaired people. I had cookery and family magazines and some library books on tape from Torch. I put this particular one at the bottom of a small pile of other wallets, which I kept on the kitchen shelf. I went about my household tasks and, as I vacuumed, saw in my mind the pile of wallets. I couldn't get the bottom one out of my mind; it began to irritate me. Finally, switching off the hoover in the hall, I went to the kitchen and removed the bottom wallet from the pile. Taking out the cassette I put it in the tape recorder and pressed 'play'. I had no idea what was on the tape, just another in a regular supply which fell through the letter box almost daily.

To my utter astonishment it was a magazine called *Torch Family News*, seemingly a newsletter about the daily work of Torch. A man's gentle voice spoke.

'Welcome to the *Torch Family News*.' Then he read a Scripture from Matthew 9:37-38 – 'The harvest is plentiful but the labourers are few . . .'

I was rooted to the spot, my cheeks flared with colour and my eyes filled with unshed tears as he went on, 'Torch is desperately in need of workers in many departments.'

I couldn't believe what I was hearing. By now, I held onto the kitchen work surface as the tears began to fall. A great warmth came over me just as it had done some time before when the Spirit of God had come upon me. I listened on as he continued to read out our joint CV.

I knew He was speaking to me but I experienced a mixture of joy and horror, too. When Peter came home I met him at the door and without a word, took him silently by the hand and led him straight to the kitchen.

'What's going on?' he queried.

I couldn't say a word. I just went straight to the cassette player and switched it on once more. We held each other, knowing that God had spoken. I shared about the ultimatum I had given God in prayer that previous Monday morning and how He had answered it so completely on the very last day.

'I can't believe I said that to Him, I felt so bad about it afterwards but I just couldn't rid my mind of thoughts about Torch. I never believed He could answer it so quickly and in such a way. That'll teach me to pray such things.' The reality of what this could mean for us was dawning on me.

'We can do it, can't we?' I looked into Peter's eyes, willing him to say something encouraging.

'Of course we can.' He hugged me tightly. 'I hope.'

We knew that this was it, what we had prayed for, a call on our lives to serve Him in full-time ministry, but this was not what we had expected or hoped for. I couldn't believe God would send me to work with the blind and Peter was shocked to think that for the first time in our life together people would say he had a blind wife.

He kept pacing the floor and saying, 'You're just Kate,

you're just my Kate, not blind or partially sighted, just my lovely wife Kate.'

It was a very hard time for us as we spent time before the Lord seeking Him about this, but we knew we had to contact Torch Trust and tell them what we believed God was saying to us; we knew we would have no peace until we had done so.

We wrote a letter to Mr and Mrs Heath, founders of the Torch Trust, just before Christmas explaining what we believed God was saying to us. We had a reply and were invited to go and visit them for the day. We of course accepted. Early in the New Year we set off, telling no one of what we were doing, as we did not want to risk anyone influencing this major decision in our lives. The thought of uprooting from the North of England was a huge undertaking for me as I had lived in the same area for all my life. I knew it so well, every turning for miles around, I could picture most places from childhood memories. I was anxious about going to somewhere completely different. However, we found our way to a small village in Leicestershire, 150 miles away, called Hallaton, passing the thatched cottages and village duck pond on our way to Torch House, headquarters of the Trust.

Torch House was originally the main Hall for the village, a large forty-roomed house with many bedrooms and some large living areas. Mr Heath showed us around; it seemed very dark to me and there were steps up and down all over the place. However, he had an obvious love and enthusiasm for the work and gentle sense of humour which really encouraged us both. We met so many people, heard so much information and, during the daily chapel meeting, had a great sense of the presence of the Lord. We talked with the Heaths and they suggested a longer stay if we felt that God was leading us forward, perhaps even returning with the girls during the school Easter holiday.

Celebrating Christmas together, Middlesbrough 1993

We travelled home with many long silences in the car as we both thought about all we had seen and heard. What should we do? What did God want us to do? Was this right? What about the girls?

We waited on the Lord for a number of weeks, eventually deciding that we had to pursue this further and so we told the children that we were going to Torch for a few days. They were excited at the prospect, as by now I had arranged to receive a children's magazine on tape, produced by Torch, called *Spark*. The girls loved it and each month heard more about the people who worked there, their homes and families and pets, too. They looked forward to meeting the people behind the voices; of course they didn't know the real reason we were going, as to tell them, without a definite idea of the future, would have been an unnecessary worry for them.

By the time we arrived at Torch, car packed up with books and games for the girls, we were eagerly anticipating what God was going to show us. We approached the front door with two excited girls and rang the bell. A young man answered the door and left us in the hallway whilst he went off to find someone to help us.

'It's a bit dark and quiet in here,' whispered Victoria, clutching tightly to my hand.

'I guess everyone is at work.' I squeezed her hand encouragingly. Nervousness was starting to affect me, too. Rebecca sniffed.

'Smells like onions,' she grimaced. 'Do you think that's for tea?'

Peter diverted their attention by pointing out the aquarium gurgling gently away in the corner; 'Let's see what we can spot in here.'

Then, footsteps. A lady appeared, we introduced ourselves and she looked at Peter and said, 'We would like to give you some experience in the various departments, so you can spend a few days in production this week and then, after the weekend, a few days in the tape department to find out where suits you best.'

She then turned to me. I waited eagerly to find out where I was to be placed.

'Of course, you will be looking after the children.'

I was so shocked. We were here as a couple, called as a couple. I couldn't believe my ears. We were shown to our family room where we unpacked and off went Peter, hugging me first as we looked at each other in bemusement.

So, here I was; strange house, strange environment and two girls to entertain for a week, not quite what I was expecting. However, rallying round, we set off to explore the village. It was very pretty with its chocolate box thatched cottages, pond and various sheep dotted about the place. The village shop supplied us with daily doses of sweets to fill the morning walks.

One afternoon, a few days into our stay, we ran back as a freak hail storm bounced ice marbles against us. Due to the change in weather, we were despatched to the laundry to help. The girls happily folded towels and sheets together, enjoying the novelty of working the motorised sheet press. I however, stood ironing all afternoon, my head buzzing with disgruntled thoughts. I could have stayed at home and ironed, what was going on? I was such an independent person at home; I cooked for the family, cleaned my home, taught in school and joined in with everything. But here I found myself sitting at Torch's dining room tables feeling very blind and helpless, something I had not felt for so long. It all began to close in on me and all I wanted to do was run away. Each night I would hide under the bedcovers and cry. I was so confused and felt so abandoned by the Lord.

I prayed, 'Lord, if you really want me here, help me, speak to me, show me, please.' Peter was struggling, not with the work but with the fact that it seemed so centred on him coming to work and me tagging along as his wife. It was not at all what God had shown us over past months, but we decided to keep trusting Him and to wait.

Two ladies in particular befriended us; they seemed to know how we were feeling and kept on telling us that we must know that we were 'called' to the work. I must admit I wondered why they kept saying this but would not find out for some time to come. They suggested that we might like to have a break and go to a local church on the Sunday evening whilst they looked after the children. We took the opportunity and off we went.

At the beginning of the service a man went out to the front and read an opening psalm, Psalm 37. A verse seemed to shout out to me, 'Be patient and wait for God to act' (verse 7 GNB). I knew God was speaking to me.

'Be patient,' I thought. 'I'd like to be, but how? Peter's doing everything and there doesn't seem to be anything for me.'

The service moved on through worship and then, when the time came to hear the sermon, the same gentleman stood and told us he was going to speak on that exact verse. So, for the next half hour, my prayer was answered. I learned how to be patient and wait for God to act! I felt much more at peace that night and the next morning, over breakfast, Mrs Heath came and asked if I would like to come to the *Spark* editorial meeting, as I had children, and my input would be helpful. I was so glad to be asked to do anything other than housework; I accepted eagerly.

Peter walked across to the editorial room with me, five minutes before the meeting was due to begin, and opened the door. He laughed as he pulled out a seat for me at the long editorial table.

'Guess what is on the banner hanging on the wall?' I couldn't think.

'Be patient and wait for God to act.' He left me quickly, still laughing. Was God beginning to show me that I, too, had a place here?

On the following Wednesday evening a visiting speaker came for the Bible study; he spoke on John 21, the very verses about the lambs and the sheep that God had spoken to us both all those months back. We began to sense God really was confirming the way to us. At the Sunday morning service held in the Torch chapel, a beautiful wood-panelled room with period fireplace (there were around forty staff living, working and worshipping together in the house at that time), the preacher stood and told us that he had a different message to bring, that he really felt that God had told him to speak on John 21, in particular 'feed my lambs'.

Peter and I looked at each other and knew the inevitable; God had surrounded this time with His Word and the way ahead seemed very clear now. There was, of course, the small matter of our children, the upheaval from our home in the north, new schools and all the readjustments. However, it seemed that perhaps God was ahead of us for, as we packed up the car to leave, the girls were asking if we could come and live at Torch. What a shock. They loved the village and as we drove away were writing down estate agents' names and numbers!

Moving cautiously forward, we began to ask God for further confirmations. He was so gracious and patient with us, He knew this was a huge move for us and so began to litter our lives with those things that would underline Torch for us. We would open magazines in doctors' waiting rooms and find ourselves looking at 'Village of the month – Hallaton'; we turned on the radio and there it was again: Hallaton. Everywhere we turned, the signpost pointed one way – Torch House. Whether it was fear or just the huge need in us to be certain we let the time run on and soon we were approaching the end of the school year. We rang our friend Bill and asked for his advice. He only laughed,

'What do you two want? Writing in the sky?'

'That would be helpful.' We laughed, too, but in truth, that was the kind of startling and impossible sign we needed.

He suggested that, in the light of all our many confirmations, we really needed to take the final step of faith and put our house up for sale. This was a time of slump as far as the housing market was concerned; many similar properties in our street had been up for sale for around eighteen months with no success. So it was with great amusement that our estate agent heard me tell her that we needed to sell within two weeks so that we could be in Leicestershire for the beginning of the new school year.

'We'll go for a week, shall we?' she replied in mocking tones. We had booked a summer holiday at Ellel Grange, where they ran a family Bible week. The girls had a wonderful time – swimming every day, a rounders match and barbeque on the huge back lawn and lots of fun with the staff running the daily Bible sessions with music, art and plenty of games.

We had only been there a few days when we received a phone call. A rather incredulous but excited estate agent was on the end of the line.

'Mrs Mancey, I had to ring you myself, I just can't believe it, we've sold your house for the full asking price – less than a week!'

'I can believe it,' I replied, 'we've been praying.'

So, there it was, the final barrier knocked firmly down. The way ahead was clear and with only a few weeks left we began to pack. We had no idea, of course, where we were going to be living and so we contacted Torch. They told us that their accommodation on the Torch site was full and so we would need to buy a house in the area, but as time was short we could stay temporarily in two down-stairs rooms of an old manse in a nearby town.

There followed a three week period of frantic activity with much clearing out of hoarded belongings. This brought us face to face with all our past, our childhood and college life, our teaching careers and music endeavours. As we dared to look into the loft, we felt that God was asking us to let go of the things of the past and to only look forward. This was not an easy time; we sat for many hours on the floor, sometimes with tears, surrounded by cardboard boxes and a large roll of black bin bags.

As we painstakingly pulled out one cardboard box after another and tore off the sellotape, much more than dust began to affect us.

'Oh my goodness, college files,' I exclaimed. 'Can you read me the covers?' I asked Peter.

I listened in amazement as he ran through the titles of assignments neatly filed away. 'History of Education', 'Music of the Baroque Period', 'Piaget's Theory of Child Development'.

'Was I really ever that intelligent?' I queried. 'It seems like someone else's life.'

'I know what you mean,' Peter mused as he thumbed through a stack of his college work. 'We're never going to use it again are we? Guess we'd better throw it away.'

We emptied the contents of the files into a black sack, the combined efforts and achievements of six years' hard work.

'Oh look!' I cried with delight, holding up a large soft blue teddy. 'The bear I made not long after I lost my sight.'

I sat cuddling it, remembering the time I had spent trying to pin and then sew up this bear. It had meant so much at the time, a first achievement of something creative to try and encourage me into thinking that I could still do things.

'He'll have to go, I don't need him.' I pushed him into the sack and continued opening boxes. A few hours later I happened to glance to my left and saw a big blue furry leg sticking out above the top of a sack. I began to cry.

'Whatever's the matter?' Peter asked, leaning across the mess and catching hold of my hand.

'It's so silly of me, but it's the bear; it took me so many weeks, unpicking sewing mistakes, re-sewing, stuffing it . . . daft of me, I know.' I wiped my eyes.

'Here.' Peter pulled out the bear and pressed him into my arms. 'Keep him. God doesn't mind,' he laughed. 'Letting go of the past is not as easy as we thought, is it?'

Why were we finding this so difficult? What did these possessions mean to us? They signified our hard work but more than that; we realised as we later sought the Lord that the reason for our finding it all so upsetting was that we had seen our value and worth in our success and achievements, which were represented in these boxes.

God wants us to be successful, that's His plan and He delights in it. However, in God's eyes we are accepted and valued just as we are, precious in His sight as His creation. He approves of us but it is our hearts that the Lord wants, not our success. We realised that we had put our value and worth in our achievements and so we disposed of these things, which after all had only been gathering dust. We began to walk on the path that God would have us all walk along, where His plans would lead to the successes He has planned for each one of us, which store up 'treasures in heaven' (Matthew 6:20).

Whilst knowing that we had some temporary accommodation near to Torch, we of course continued to seek the Lord for a house of our own. We were on the mailing lists of estate agents in the area but as we began to look we realised that house prices in the north of England varied greatly to those in the Leicestershire area. We saw ourselves living in a tent in the Torch grounds, but God's view of things far outstretched our small seed of faith. He was about to begin to teach us the first of many lessons of His provision as 'Jehovah Jireh', God our provider. We were to learn that He really can do 'immeasurably more than all we ask or imagine' (Ephesians 3:20 NIV).

During our waiting time a dear old man in our church, called Fred, came to us and told us very specifically that we should be praying for a four bedroomed detached house, as God had shown him that we would have many people staying with us. I must admit that we did laugh at such a suggestion. Our little bungalow to a detached house and the colossal difference in national house prices? It wasn't possible. However, we respected him as a man of God and, crazy though it seemed, began to pray, asking God for just that.

Our further request was that it would be a house of peace, as one of the most specific blessings visitors to our home would comment upon was the peace they found in our home. This 'peace' must have been God's peace (John 14:27), as in the natural sense, with two young girls and all the busy comings and goings we experienced each day, our house could not be described as peaceful! The third request was for a garden large enough to build a dog run for my now third guide-dog, Axel.

Estate agents' sheets came and only made it to the bin. We were getting quite desperate but went on praying each day, making our requests known to God (Philippians 4:6). One morning we opened an envelope and there again were a number of agent's information sheets.

'Is there one with four bedrooms?' I eagerly enquired as Peter browsed through them. This was such a frustrating part of my life as a partially sighted person, to have everyone else read the post first.

'Just the one.' My hope rose once again.

'Never mind looking at all the front stuff.' I snatched up the sheet, turned it over and gave it back to Peter. 'Just see if it has a garden.'

I sat as patiently as I could and then Peter began to laugh.

'What is it?' How annoying, he'd seen something, what was it? He began to read, 'The house has a garden with a built in dog run!'

For years now we have shared this story of God's confirmation and not one person has ever come across such a thing in an estate agent's sheet before.

As we drove down to see this house, God gave us a Scripture to look at. We visited the house first as time was tight and knew instantly that this was God's choice for us. As we sat by a nearby reservoir munching on fish and chips, we remembered the Scripture reference. To our astonishment, when we looked it up in our Bible, the paragraph was headed 'The Glory of the New House', and went on to talk about the peace of this house being greater than that of the former one (Haggai 2:9). What more was there to say? All three requests answered.

There was only one drawback – the price. We were fifty thousand pounds short of the asking price but God had confirmed through His Word that this was the house for us and so we asked Him to show us what to do. It's the human thing to expect to have to 'do' something, as if we could help God out. Once again, He had gone ahead of us and put someone across our path just a short time before. We didn't mention our need to anyone but we were offered fifty thousand pounds as a gift towards our move. The exact amount needed to complete the purchase! ' "The silver is mine, and the gold is mine," declares the LORD of hosts' (Haggai 2:8).

Although our house was sold, the paperwork had still to be finalised and so we stacked our belongings in one room of our bungalow and began to squash all we could into our car. We were leaving with the minimum of belongings to tide us over until we could ship everything else down. The morning came to leave and we found ourselves with a backseat full of bags and boxes and two girls, one younger one excited about the journey and a grumpy teenager, who now far from wanted to leave her home and friends in the north. We recalled sharing our concerns about the girls with a friend who told us that God would deal with all of our move, including the children. Although God loves us individually, He does not call us and expect our families to just 'drag along behind'. He loves and cares for the whole picture and has a specific, tailor made plan for each one of us. Just as not one of us is created by accident, not one of us is where we find ourselves by accident either, if we love Him with all our heart. We certainly needed His assurance and help and so we silently prayed that God would bring His peace as we set out for Leicestershire.

I'm not sure what we were expecting, but what we found didn't live up to our expectations. We collected the key and directions from Torch House and drove straight over to the manse. We let ourselves in through the old front door and entered a very dark and cold house. The girls went ahead and returned to us dismayed. They had found two rooms; one, which would be theirs, with just enough room for two mattresses on the floor and a plastic crate full of their books and games, and the other with a further two single beds and a wardrobe. We were to share the kitchen with a lady living on the upper floor; Joan was very welcoming when she arrived home from work and helped us to settle in.

We sat together that night, Peter and I in chairs, the girls on the beds, and prayed that Jesus would help us. We were tired, cold and wondering just what we had done. We asked God for His peace and yet again put our trust in

Him. Putting the girls to bed I had many thoughts running through my mind. This was our new life, our exciting adventure with Christ . . . not quite what we were expecting or had hoped for. Perhaps, I thought, this was why the two ladies had insisted that we knew we were called to the work.

As the next two weeks unfolded, we all caught colds and had tummy upsets; it was grim and we had to begin work the following week and get the children into school. We gathered our family together in our room once again and Peter served us communion as we asked Jesus to pour in His strength. We hung on to the only thing we knew for sure – God had called us and He promised in His Word that if we were to seek first His Kingdom and all His righteousness, then 'all these things will be added to you' (Matthew 6:33). There was no going back now; only forward.

EIGHT

Faith, Fun and Fellowship

The girls soon settled into school life and made new friends and we began working a few days later. There was a wonderful sense of God's presence as the whole staff met together daily in the chapel room at Torch House. These people had such a love for God and for visually impaired people and their greatest desire was to get the Word of God into as many hands as possible through the literature, which was produced in Braille, giant print and on cassette. Peter began his work in the tape department as an editor. This entailed receiving books from home workers, which had been read on reel-to-reel tape. His daily work was to listen to the recordings while following the script in the print book, cutting out any errors using his trusty razor blade and then inserting re-recorded corrections. He loved this work; as an avid reader this was pure bliss, reading all day! Today, the recordings are made on disc and edited on computer.

I was taken along to a small prefabricated hut on the perimeter of the site which was called Aid Africa, as half of the area was full of boxes of clothing, towels and flannels, soaps and other aid which would be sorted and regularly despatched overseas in containers. The other half of the building was devoted to the copying of cassette magazines bound for Africa. The Torch Trust produces magazines in their recording studios specifically for overseas listeners as well as the UK. Many thousands of copies are sent bi-monthly and are eagerly awaited, some readers walking many hours to collect their magazines from the post office in remote parts of their country.

We heard many testimonies of how these magazines are shared among friends and Braille copies read over and over again until the Braille dots simply wear away; of groups of friends coming to know the Lord Jesus just through His Word – it is truly the living Word for them. I spent my time fast-copying these cassette magazines; at that time those registered for overseas numbered around three thousand. Each cassette needed to be labelled and checked for sound quality before they were packed and posted.

For the first few months, I worked alone and after only a few weeks I realised that this could be my area of service for years to come. No matter how I tried to vary my system of work it was very tedious and repetitive; thousands of tapes loomed ahead of me and the repetition of the same piece of music and words when checking the beginning of each tape began to irritate me greatly. There is, of course, in any work a place for determination and endurance, doing the best we can in that particular job. However, our Lord also wants us to be living in peace and joy. I recall standing with my hands on the tape copiers one morning in my second week and praying aloud,

'If this is what you have for me, Lord, then please give me your peace in order to do it.' Immediately an overwhelming peace came upon me; I stood in God's presence for many minutes as He ministered patience and a love for what I was doing into me.

When I met Peter on the driveway to leave for home that day, I grinned broadly at him over the car roof. He knew what a struggle I had been having.

'It's all right now,' I said, 'I can stay!'

We moved into our new home on November 5th, 1994 and, in the midst of cardboard boxes and general chaos, celebrated with hot dogs, tomato soup and fireworks in the garden. We couldn't believe that we were to live in this, what seemed to us to be a mansion of a home, with its beautiful peaceful situation. The girls began to unpack their boxes and make their bedrooms their own and we prepared our home for the promised visitors. Who would they be and what did the future hold? We had no answers to these questions but began to realise that this walk of faith was something totally different to what we had ever experienced in our lives before.

My little Aid Africa hut was a cold spot in winter and I was glad to go across to the staff coffee bar mid-morning to defrost and enjoy many crazy times together with the young helpers we had staying at Torch from overseas. The language caused many a humorous moment and dictionaries were in full operation most of the time. I recall Ikuko, a young lady from Japan, one break time sniffing the air.

'What are we having for lunch?'

'Beef casserole,' we chorused.

'Beef? What is that?'

'Cow,' we replied. She hesitated for a moment and then rifled through her dictionary, letting out an exclamation of horror as she found the translation she had been searching for.

'Oh no!' she screeched.

'What's the matter?' we enquired.

'Elephant, you're eating elephant!'

We all burst into laughter as she stood making her arm into a trunk to explain. Something was seriously wrong with the translation and we quickly reassured her we were certainly not having elephant casserole for lunch!

This young lady had somehow found her way to Torch

House, thinking that we were an English-teaching house
– 'Teachy House'! She was assigned to work with me and
one morning my much prayed for opportunity to share the
gospel with her came. I had put on a cassette of Christian
worship. She loved music.

'What is this?' she enquired.

'It's music about Jesus.' I smiled across the desk at her.

'Jesus?' She sounded puzzled. 'Is he a singer?'

We can never know when or how the opportunity will
arise to share our wonderful message of God's love or who
God will bring across our paths. We got to know these
young people very well and began to invite them into our
home; the girls loved it and learned much about many
different cultures. We found Victoria one day walking
around the house balancing my only cut glass trifle dish
on her head, practising to be like Sekina from the Comoros
Islands, whom she had seen walking down the corridor,
her hands full, carrying a bowl of fruit on her head. They
learned wedding dances and tried, what were to us,
strange foods as we all made lifelong friendships.

We had a desire in us to open up our home more to
these youngsters and also to the staff who lived in Torch
House itself and thought that perhaps a Bible study once
a week would be a good way of beginning. We also had
contact with a supplier of some excellent Christian films
on video and thought that perhaps every other week we
could watch a film together. As our weeks were already
quite busy and because we only had a small portable television in our living room and it would be impossible for
folks to see that small screen, I asked the Lord to confirm
this idea of a weekly get together by providing us with a
suitable sized television. We had no savings and no money
with which to buy one ourselves but we knew God could
provide for us if this was the right thing to do.

Four days later, during the afternoon as I was cleaning

the house, the door bell rang and a lady I had met fairly recently stood on the doorstep rather anxiously.

'May I come in?' she faltered. I wondered what was the matter as she took a seat.

'I hope you won't be offended,' she began.

'Goodness,' I thought, 'what is she about to say?' My mind raced. Surely we couldn't have done anything to upset her; we hardly knew her.

'I have a large colour television in my car that has been given away, would you like it?' she said.

Imagine my excitement and astonishment; she knew nothing about my secret prayer, no one did. I told her what I had prayed just that week and how God had used her to confirm our way ahead. We went out to the car and literally staggered into the dining room, depositing what seemed to me to be a huge television on the dining room table. When Peter came home I could hardly contain myself as I took him by the hand.

'You'll never guess what's in the dining room. Come on.'

Knowing nothing about my secret prayer either, he too was astonished. He looked into the living room at our television cabinet in which stood our 'pea on a drum' portable and said, 'It'll never fit, it's too big.'

I was horrified and said, 'It must fit, it will fit, God's sent it.' So, with great trepidation we carried it across and slid it onto the shelf with not a paper width to spare at either side. How amazing is our Lord!

Thus began many years of the most wonderful evenings in our home. We had great times of worship, Bible study, fellowship and were both challenged and entertained by many films, including *The Hiding Place*, *The Cross and the Switchblade* and on one unforgettable evening the story of Jackie Pullinger, a lady whom God has used to bring His complete freedom to many hundreds of drug addicts in Hong Kong.

Our room was full that evening and just before the film

began we asked that at the end no one would talk, as was usual, for we wanted to allow God to speak to us. We had seen snippets of the film early that morning before rushing out to work and knew it was very powerful. Indeed it was, our amazing Lord was touching lives in incredible ways and the testimonies of these people were astonishing. The film finished and silence descended. The presence of the Lord was tangible and across the room I heard someone begin to quietly cry.

I silently prayed, 'Oh Jesus, touch their life. I don't know who it is but they need you.' Suddenly there was a loud shout, a cry of deep pain and one of the young men shot backwards across the room and began to sob. At the same moment as his anguished cry rang out, the electricity sourcing the ground floor sockets blew.

We were plunged into darkness as the lamps went out. A tumult of prayer began. Victoria ran out to the utility room where the fuse box was mounted on the wall and came running back to tell us, somewhat puzzled, that the trip switches were still all in place! Some minutes later the lights came back on and the kettle in the kitchen began to boil again, totally unaided by us. The power of the Holy Spirit had been so strong it had blown the electricity, which was then supernaturally restored.

There was such excitement amongst us all. Peter and I crawled across the floor to minister God's love to this young man's pain; his family's past had involved drug abuse and God was healing and delivering him from much hurt and pain that had held him over many years. As God ministered to him the rest of the house was filled with joyous singing and rejoicing in the goodness of God, led by Samuel, a captain in the Uganda Church Army, who happened to be visiting Torch at that time.

That young man went on from strength to strength in the Lord, finally leaving Torch to spend a number of years with another Christian training organisation, including three months serving in India. He is now married and settled in London, working with a Christian mission.

Whilst talking over cups of tea and coffee one evening at house group, our girls mentioned they were going to a 'sleepover' that weekend.

'A sleepover?' the group queried, 'What's a sleepover?'

The girls explained, and the others thought it sounded fun and that they would have liked to have had that experience themselves in their younger days.

'You're never too old for a sleepover,' we said.

'Can we have one, Mummy?' the girls pleaded.

'Why not?' we thought, 'It's never too late to try anything.'

So, there we were a few weeks later, around fifteen of us; men downstairs, the ladies up, strewn about the house on sofas and floors, sleeping bags a-plenty, and for the very fortunate, a bed! We went swimming, watched a film and ate fish and chips and the next morning went off to our church. These were great times that we were to repeat.

On one weekend we went by minibus to Wembley Stadium where there was a huge gathering of Christians. The event was named 'Champion of the World' and was hosted by Noel Richards, a renowned Christian musician. It was a most amazing experience for us all; around fifty thousand Christians gathered together to join in worshipping the Lord with various contemporary worship bands and solo artists – Delirious, Matt Redman, Sue Rinaldi and many others. It began at four in the afternoon and went on until around nine that evening. Our young people and daughters went down onto the pitch and danced the day away before the Lord; the sound of all those thousands of people chanting the name of Jesus was truly awesome, a day that will remain with us all.

God taught me much about hospitality during that

time, about how to give of our time, possessions and effort unstintingly, trusting Him for all we need. The Holy Spirit was teaching me much about servanthood, right down to the finer details. I recall having washed and ironed the spare room bedding for the umpteenth time that month. Somewhat weary, I remembered that we had recently stayed in someone's home where they simply put a sheet under the duvet cover, I guessed to save time and effort on washing and ironing.

'Great idea,' I mused and was about to set off to find two single sheets to adopt this idea. However, I heard the Spirit say to me,

'Aren't my guests worth the extra effort it takes to wash and iron two duvet covers each time?'

Stopped in my tracks and admonished there and then, I realised that I was short-changing our houseguests and have always remembered that lesson in serving with our whole heart.

There were other lessons in doing a thorough job and walking in excellence in even the seemingly small matters. I found the Holy Spirit causing me to notice dropped clothing items under my feet whilst shopping.

I was thinking, 'Oh, messy people,' but the Lord said to me, 'You pick them up then.'

In the supermarket when choosing a bag of frozen peas the neatly stacked pile slid to one side. I walked away unconcerned only to be nudged by the Spirit once again to return and neatly stack them back as they were, after all, someone had spent their time making a good job of it. Even around the house the Lord was teaching me to be thorough in all I was doing, as, if we cultivate an attitude of excellence in the little things, then this will spill over into our service for Him. I am far from perfect in this but as we remain open to His prompting He will show us what it is He requires in order to equip us for all He has set ahead in the future.

NINE

Led by the Spirit

As a family, we have been blessed with the gift of music and as a result were invited to many places to minister. We found ourselves on numerous weekends, the car stuffed from top to bottom, front to back, not only with suitcases and games and books and picnic for the journey but guitars, violin, recorders and congas – huge drums with which our younger daughter added wonderful rhythms to everything we played. There was also a small space kept in the corner of the boot for my guide dog; Axel was a much taller dog who seemed to be able to fold himself up into a tiny ball when necessary.

By now, of course, he was retired as my partial sight had caused me not to put my full trust in him when out and about, an essential for working a dog. I would use the sight I had which, when approaching busy roads would make me nervously slow him down and, sensing my lack of trust, he began to waver in his work. Having been used to being with me at all times, I took him into work just on the lead and he lay contentedly under my desk, thumping his tail enthusiastically on the floor as visitors to my office stopped for a stroke.

Torch House hosted house parties at Christmas, Easter and during the summer months. They were a full week, for families, twenties or those slightly older folks. With two of the most accomplished musicians from the Torch staff, David and Trevor, we led some of the worship times each morning and evening, Rebecca with her beautiful violin playing, Victoria skilfully providing rhythm on the congas and drum kit and Peter and myself with guitar and recorders. We knew wonderful times of God's presence, peace and joy.

It was a few days before a deputation weekend in the winter that God stepped in once again, this time showing His protection for His children and ability to forewarn us of dangers ahead. I had a vivid dream from God on Tuesday night. In it, I stood at the end of a road and watched as Peter set off in the car, the girls in the back seat. I waved goodbye but to my horror as they were heading away, the car swerved off to the left, rolled over and burst into flames.

I woke up and God said to me, 'Check the brakes.' I woke Peter and shared the dream with him; it had really shaken me. We contacted our local garage as soon as it opened that morning and took it in before work. They put it up on the ramps and the mechanic exclaimed in horror at what he saw. Apparently the brake pipes had corroded and fluid was leaking from them onto the brakes themselves.

'In effect, you have no brakes,' he told us. The car was repaired that day and as we drove on the motorway that Saturday, the rain was pouring and the traffic heavy. We praised God for His love and protection over us as we real-ised what could have happened under such bad driving conditions and how the Lord had kept us safe: 'The Lord will keep your going out and your coming in from this time forth and for evermore' (Psalm 121:8).

We had the opportunity to record a family CD for Torch. We wanted our music to bring blessing to others and were, of course, keen to have a record of our family whilst we were all together, as the girls were growing up so quickly and music was a central part of our lives and brought us a lot of fun as well as hard work.

The recording took place up in Middlesbrough, our home ground. What an experience that was. Recorded on the hottest of summer days, we spent the time melting over our instruments, headphones on, trying not to swallow the microphones encased in large sponge covers, placed there to cut down any extraneous sounds. It was really exacting at times, something of which we had no experience. Each instrument had to be recorded separately and we were most impressed with our girls: Rebecca improvising expertly as ever and Victoria, who, with great concentration, played her way through whole songs on the drum kit with exact timing, even to slowing up precisely at the end of songs. We knew at that point she was going to make an excellent drummer and Rebecca, five years older, was already proving herself a superb violinist. We found ourselves on many occasions in fits of giggles as we tried to put instrumental parts in part way through a song; I was a nervous wreck! However, some weeks later we found ourselves excitedly receiving the first copy of our CD, *I Know a Place*.

As part of our outreach work with Torch and also through our church fellowship we were invited to share testimony and had the privilege of praying after meetings with many people. There are a few meetings that particularly stand out in my mind as God moved in people's lives in most extraordinary ways. We never know when the power of God will touch people, we can only go on being obedient to His command to share the good news of Jesus Christ and expect signs and wonders to follow the preaching of the Word, as the Scripture says, 'Go into all the world and proclaim the gospel . . . And these signs will accompany those who believe . . .' (Mark 16:15-17).

After one meeting in a church in Leicestershire the Holy Spirit gave us some 'words of knowledge' (1 Corinthians 12:8); one was 'mothballs.' I found myself standing in front of the church arguing with the Lord in my head.

'This can't be you God, can it?' I was hesitating. 'It's so ridiculous, I must be making it up. . . . What will they think . . . ?'

However, past experience told me that I shouldn't rely on my own thinking but just be obedient and so I gave out the word. To my utter astonishment a gentleman came out to the front in tears. God had spoken to him and reminded him that he had not followed a calling He had given to him many years ago. He had put God's plans for him into mothballs. He came out wanting to repent and receive God's forgiveness and allow the Lord to re-commission him again for the work he should have done when first called by Him. To see the joy in that man when the Lord had ministered restoration to him was wonderful. He had lifted off him the disappointment and sense of failure and replaced it with hope for the future and great love.

In another meeting we prayed for various people who had needs and were just generally talking with people after the service had finished. A young man was telling us that he was getting married in a few months time and that his fiancée was there too; she was Holly and they were both students at local universities. We asked if we could pray for God's blessing on them in their future. He went off to get her. After we had prayed for them, I started to chat to Holly and asked her what she was studying. I can't recall now what it was she was currently studying to become except that she told me she had always wanted to go into nursing but because of her back she couldn't, and so had found an alternative second best.

'God never wants second best for any of us,' I said. 'Can we pray for you?' She was keen for this, if not somewhat surprised. We sat down. She told me that she was born with this problem and had never been able to sit up straight. That was all she said. So, I prayed and asked God to minister His healing power into her back. She sat straight up.

'I can sit up straight!' she exclaimed in delight, 'I can't believe it!' It was the first time she had been able to do this for twenty and more years. We exchanged telephone numbers as she was so excited, especially with her forthcoming wedding. However, that was not the end of God's miraculous work in her life. Two days later she rang me.

'Kate, about my back,' she said. Sad to say, doubt hit my mind instantly and I thought something had gone wrong; God really was teaching me about remaining in faith and trusting Him.

'You know near the bottom of your spine it curves in?' she continued. I found myself holding the phone with one hand and feeling the base of my spine with the other.

'Yes,' I tentatively replied.

'Well, I've just been getting changed and standing side on to the mirror and I've seen this curve. I've never had one before, you see, I didn't tell you the other evening but I had the bottom three vertebrae missing and now they've grown back!'

There was much joy that evening in our home as I shared this amazing news at the dinner table. Three weeks later we took a carload of young people to a Delirious concert in Leicester and to our surprise met Holly; she was so excited as, for the first time in her life, she had danced the night away before the Lord!

Learning to be obedient when given spiritual gifts from the Lord has often been a nerve-racking but very exciting experience. The Bible teaches us that these gifts are a normal part of our Christian life, we should expect them: 'Now there are varieties of gifts, but the same Spirit . . .

to each is given the manifestation of the Spirit for the common good. . . . All these are empowered by one and the same Spirit, who apportions to each one individually as he wills' (1 Corinthians 12:4, 7, 11).

I think, as in many things, God must have been testing me out to see how much I really trusted Him, as during one meeting a number of words of knowledge came into my mind. Once again I found myself doubting that these could possibly be from the Lord, and I had stayed quiet on past occasions and then heard someone else in the service give out the same words. I was beginning to learn just to say what He was telling me to. If we don't, He will get His work done somehow. He is never stuck and will always find someone else more willing to risk being obedient – very humbling.

Two of these words were 'ambulance' and 'changing rooms'. I tentatively gave them out, excusing myself as I did, to save face, I guess, just in case they were wrong. How many times God must sigh over me but He is so patient and I am now learning to 'just give them'. Immediately, two people responded. The Holy Spirit had shown them just why these words were for them and what He wanted to do for them.

A gentleman came to the front and shared with me that God had reminded him of a frantic and frightening ambulance ride when he was a very small child. He relived the sound of the siren and the flashing blue light in his pain. This journey had allowed a fear of hospitals and sickness to come into him, which, forty years later, he was still grappling with. As we prayed, he wept just as a small boy and God graciously took away his fear.

The 'changing rooms' was for a lady who told me that she was never able to settle; every time she got things right, with much effort and care, she became immediately dissatisfied with it and changed it again. She worked her way around her house, much to the frustration of her family. God ministered His love and rest into her heart and mind and put a depth of His presence into her so that she needed only to turn to Him for her stability and to know He would meet all her needs. She was so overwhelmed by His peace and rest.

Our God is so amazing, He knows just what will trigger our thoughts and touch our innermost needs. God used a gift of knowledge to speak into my own life as I found myself seeking Him for a change of role in Torch. The work I was doing in Aid Africa was coming to an end and, at the same time, the current receptionist was also leaving the work. I was approached to see if I would pray about taking on this new role. I was very anxious about this having never done anything of this kind before; many doubts about my own ability crowded my mind and I really needed to know what God would have me do, as I knew His choice always worked out best for me.

We were going to a family Bible week with a group of Christians during the summer and as part of the teaching time, we split into small groups and asked the Lord to teach us about receiving words of knowledge for each other. I silently asked the Lord to speak to me about my future work. A gentleman in my group said he had a word for me, though he had no idea what on earth it could possibly mean.

'It's an elephant,' he sheepishly shared. 'Perhaps you're to go to Africa or India?'

'Trunk call!' I exclaimed excitedly. ('Trunk call' used to be the name given to a long distance telephone call).

The group looked at me as if I was mad. 'Trunk call?'

I explained the old joke I knew from being a little girl about an elephant making a trunk call. I knew immediately that God was confirming to me the work as receptionist, which involved mostly working with the telephone. They really couldn't see how I had come to this conclusion but when I excitedly asked Peter at coffee time what he would think of if I said 'elephant', he replied,

'Trunk call, of course.'

No wonder God's best for us as couples, as the Word expresses it, is to be equally yoked in Christ. For in married life together he can bring us to a place of oneness where we can love, laugh, encourage and be such a great blessing to each other.

He is also a God who is just and will not see His children unjustly treated. This was brought home forcibly to me one Saturday afternoon as we went into Kettering, a local town, to find some much needed clothes for the girls. Victoria was excited as she had some birthday money given to her as a gift to spend. She had spent part of it and had three pound coins left. She held on tightly to them and insisted on taking them with her into the changing rooms. I waited by the exit door and eventually both girls appeared. Victoria was extremely upset.

'I've lost my money, Mummy,' she cried. 'I dropped it and it rolled under the curtain and when I looked for it, it had gone.'

She had seen two girls laughing at her outside the changing cubicles; she asked them if they had seen her money but they only sneered and said no. She knew they had picked it up and it meant a lot to her but there was nothing she could do. I was upset for her, of course, but said that I was sure that Jesus would replace it. I didn't know how soon that was going to happen or how amazingly the Lord would accomplish that statement of faith.

The girls queued up to purchase their clothes and I stood further back, as it was extremely busy. As I waited the Holy Spirit said to me, 'There are two girls standing just behind you, they have Victoria's money.'

I was so shocked but there it was, that racing heartbeat

and I knew that the Lord was with me. Despite this knowledge I began to wrestle with myself. What if they weren't the same girls, after all, I couldn't see their reactions. What would they think? What if their parents were with them? I was so scared but felt the Lord continue to push me. Taking a small seed of courage in both hands, I turned around and said to two young teenagers, 'I think you have my daughter's money.'

Even as I began to speak, one of them was opening her purse and as I held out my hand she placed three pound coins in it. I thanked them and told them that Jesus loved them and He saw everything. Only God knows what impact that situation will have on their lives in the future but I'm sure, like me, they will never forget it.

During a church service, God gave me a picture of a huge snake, around eight feet long, very thick and dark. It had a huge head and an extremely large gaping mouth. I shared this with the church and the Holy Spirit told me, as it were, to hold it up in front of everyone. Anyone who was held captive by the devil, represented by the snake, addicted or bound in any way to anything, was to come out and God was going to set them free supernaturally. There was a real sense of urgency about it, a moment in time when God held back the enemy in order that He might set the captives free: 'The Spirit of the Lord God is upon me . . . to proclaim liberty to the captives, and the opening of the prison to those who are bound' (Isaiah 61:1).

A number of people responded to this and one man in particular came excitedly to see me after the service. He had been addicted to alcohol and had felt he must go to the front and respond to God's prompting as his greatest desire was to be set free. He told me that he saw himself pouring drink down the snake's throat, pouring his drink addiction down the enemy's throat, and that he felt set free. Over a year later I spoke to him again and he told me with great delight that now, he could go to bed at night whenever he wanted to; he no longer spent his time sitting drinking in order to get to bed and that he could freely live his life once more. God had indeed set him free.

God tells us that wisdom is a gift and that He freely gives it: 'If any of you lacks wisdom, let him ask God, who gives generously to all without reproach, and it will be given him' (James 1:5). As we seek Him in all kinds of situations we can expect Him to work, even in the most unexpected ways.

This was brought home to me when our eldest daughter, Rebecca, travelled home with a friend from the north of England. They managed to get lost at least twice, phoning home from various telephone boxes en route for further directions, arriving home in the early hours of the morning and going straight off to bed. The next morning they were up early to leave for a visit to London. As we went onto the drive to wave them off I asked Becki if she had everything.

'My wallet!' she exclaimed. 'It isn't in my jacket.'

Thus began a thorough search of bedroom, hall, car and clothing. She was most upset as not only did her wallet contain her spending money for her trip but it also contained her valuable student railcard, Boots card and her house keys. We prayed together and asked the Lord to help us retrieve this wallet, though we knew that as they had stopped in a number of places it was fairly impossible.

'Don't let it spoil your time away,' we said, smiling as we ushered them towards the car, 'It will work out.' Off they drove and I went into the living room and sat down in the armchair.

'You know where Becki's wallet is, Lord, please show me. You know we can't afford to replace everything.'

I sat quietly for a while knowing that prayer is a two way conversation and being a talkative kind of person, I have to discipline myself to give Him time to speak. I suddenly thought about the phone calls and felt a strong urge to go to the phone and see if the last incoming number from Becki's phone call had been stored. It had and though I had no idea where the area code was from, pressed the ring back button. By now, I was getting excited; I just knew God was in this situation, but how?

The phone rang and I prayed, 'Please let a Christian answer it.'

Crazy request? Then a lady picked up the phone, sounding most surprised that it had rung just as she stepped into the telephone box.

'Hello?' she tentatively said. I felt rather foolish as I explained about my daughter's travels and the loss of her wallet.

'It's not here,' she said, 'but wait a moment and I'll go into the services and enquire for you and call you back.'

A few moments later she rang back. 'They haven't got it but I'll pray for you to find it.'

'Are you a Christian?' I asked, not believing what I was hearing.

She was. I told her all that had gone on and as we talked it transpired that she was the author of a couple of books we had recorded onto tape for use in the Torch library. She was travelling to her daughter's home and was late and so had tried two previous telephone boxes *en route* but both were broken and so, in desperation, had tried a third, just at the right moment. When I told her of my prayer she, too, was most excited and we agreed to pray together, knowing that somehow God was in this with us.

Two days later the local bank rang. 'Is that the home of Rebecca Mancey?' they enquired, 'We have her wallet; it has been sent to us anonymously.'

We collected it and found that, strangely, only the Boots card was missing. Becki was thrilled to have it back and we praised God. That same week a brown envelope came through the post, no explanatory letter inside – only the Boots card! God is interested in restoring every last detail. He always completes whatever He begins.

As a wonderful and patient teacher our Lord knows just how much we can handle at one time and gently leads us forward from one experience to another. He only requires that we daily submit to Him and seek His face. These words of knowledge were the stepping stones for me to be stretched even further by God, in faith, to receive and bring words of prophecy in my home church, in nearby Stamford, where the use of spiritual gifts are encouraged. Whilst reading in the Word about the spiritual gifts I found that it said we are to 'eagerly desire the spiritual gifts, especially that you may prophesy' (1 Corinthians 14:1).

So I did. This brought about yet more terrifying but wonderful experiences, which bring not only responsibility to stick close to Him but also great joy when experiencing His anointing. There is no more wonderful place to be than in the presence of God and under His anointing. This again is a place He desires us all to be, a place open to all who seek Him wholeheartedly ('Serve wholeheartedly, as if serving the Lord, not men' Ephesians 6:7 NIV). I have fought many battles in my mind and flesh when waiting to bring a prophetic word. I wrestle with such thoughts as,

'What if I go out to the front and then forget everything?'

'What if I start to speak and then don't have anything else to say?'

'What if it's all wrong and I get into trouble?'

These all stem from the fear of man, of course, and there is only One we need to rightly fear (have reverence for) and that is the Lord Himself. The devil does not want any words of encouragement or exhortation to be given to the church from God. So there are also occasions where the enemy attempts to confuse our minds.

I remember one Sunday morning God clearly giving me the beginning of a prophetic word which said, 'Just as Moses stood before the burning bush . . .' Immediately I questioned myself, I heard the thought, 'Don't be ridiculous, it wasn't Moses – it was Joseph and the burning bush. If you give that word, they'll all know you're really stupid, you'd better stay quiet.'

I stood and thought and thought, even recalling a drawing of whoever it was, standing in front of a red crayoned bush I must have drawn in junior school. In despair I tapped Peter on the arm.

'Who stood in front of the burning bush?' I knew he looked at me as if I was crackers.

'Moses,' he said with a question in his voice.

'Hmmm,' I thought, 'nice try, Devil.'

Of course all these fears are really the fear of being humiliated, looking foolish or being reprimanded by authority in front of others, which is so ridiculous. So, as I wait on the Lord when He is nudging me to speak out I have to tell myself that there is only one I need be concerned about and that is God Himself. He is very gracious towards me, for as I begin to wrestle in my mind, His presence comes upon me and I feel something like I imagine the onset of a heart attack to be; a racing and thudding heart and I feel that if I don't give out this word I will explode! This does help to propel me to the front! It is for Him to use us for His purposes and for us just to be obedient to whatever He is asking us to do. Of course we need to come under the authority of our church leaders and have these things tested, for the safeguarding of others, but this is all part of learning to live in the Word.

The enemy, too, in our general daily living would have us all stopped in our tracks. He will use anyone and any situation. He will take full advantage of any opportunity we give him ('give no opportunity to the devil' Ephesians

4:27). The Bible prepares us for this and gives us the answers, weapons of warfare to combat everything that comes against us (*see* Ephesians 6:10-18). Knowing the Scriptures is vital in our walk with God as, in a crisis, the Holy Spirit can only bring to our minds those verses that we have put into us ('be transformed by the renewal of your mind' Romans 12:2).

I have faced many battles in my Christian life and God's promises have kept me. God knows how the stresses and events of life can rob us of our peace and joy if we allow them to. However, the Bible tells us that 'no weapon fashioned against you shall succeed' (Isaiah 54:17).

My visual impairment can so easily cause me to back away from new opportunities, but I know that 'I can do all things through Him who strengthens me'(Philippians 4:13). My greatest desire is to be able to read normal print; anything else, I'm afraid, is just not the same as holding a book in your own hands, smelling that wonderful fresh print aroma and turning the pages for yourself. At the moment I use a combination of Braille and audio to read the Word. It's far more time consuming, frustrating and certainly not as easy as it would be to just lift up a book and see the words before my eyes, but I know I need to do this for God to speak to me, encourage and direct me as well as bring me words of comfort and help when I need them.

It's true, as I step out and trust Him He proves it to me again and again. I struggled for most of my early life with a lack of confidence; especially when with groups of people an overwhelming shyness would come over me, an inability to make conversation with people. My lack of sight has given me greater courage to speak out God's message as I can't see their reactions and so I press on regardless. However, in general times of social gathering it is really difficult. My concentration needs to be on full alert as there is, of course, no eye contact. A feeling of clumsiness washes over me as I inadvertently cut across conversations or reply to questions that were never aimed at me. These moments only add to the feelings of vulnerability and stupidity. Eating out, too, can be another difficult area.

In the early days of my sight loss, I struggled valiantly to continue using a knife and fork in order to look like everyone else. Meal times used to be all about enjoying the company around me but now had become a marathon in concentration. Chasing the elusive serving of peas around my dinner plate. Never being quite sure which part of my meal I was about to eat next. The inevitable dropping of various bits of food, precariously balanced on my fork end only to fall in my lap, leaving traces of gravy as they fell. This was no fun and certainly added to a loss of dignity. It led me to use a spoon instead.

It was quite a courageous step to take; it singled me out as different but weighed up against actually being able to relax and enjoy the company I was with rather than having to spend my time concentrating on eating and coping with the embarrassment of making a mess, was well worth it. Sadly, I have met numbers of visually impaired people across the years who are still intimidated through the attitudes of others into struggling on with knife and fork. I have shared my liberation with them, which in its turn, has freed them, with great relief and pleasure, into enjoying meal times once again.

As we continued trusting God for all our needs, Peter and I often found ourselves with no earthly way of meeting our household bills. But we could rest in the certain knowledge that His Word is true and that 'my God will meet every need of yours according to His riches in glory in Christ Jesus' (Philippians 4:19). So many times we have known a large bill appear in the post for an unexpected car breakdown or household utility and that very same day another envelope reveals a gift to match the necessary amount needed.

In times when our food supply has been extremely low, we have been given gifts of freezer food, home baking and eggs from a chicken farm. The timing of these gifts was always perfect and causes us also to be alert to the prompting of His voice to give to others generously.

I firmly believe as we live according to His Word and His commands He will fulfil His promises, not always as immediately or even in the way we would desire or expect, but His timing is perfect for each individual. Some of these testing times, these wilderness experiences, are God's way of showing and proving to us that He is totally to be depended upon for everything.

God has challenged us to continue to tithe our income throughout hard times of lack, as His Word teaches us to do (Malachi 3:10), and to give over and above this to those in need. This has not always been easy and I can recall times when I have stood and cried in a shopping centre as we haven't been able to provide the clothes or shoes that I would have liked to for the girls. But somehow, in His perfect timing, He has, having proved our ongoing trust in Him, provided for our every need and more.

One day, whilst travelling home from work, we were listening to the news on the car radio. We heard that our building society was giving cash windfalls to its long term customers as part of its transition to becoming a bank. What excitement! We parked the car. I turned to Peter with the glimmer of a smile on my face.

'I suppose we could just save the money and pay off the household bills as they arrive, or . . .'

Peter held my gaze.

'We could go back to Switzerland?' he suggested.

We hugged. Our prayers had been answered in such an unexpected way. Since being healed, I had wanted to return to Switzerland with Peter and the girls, this time travelling free from anxiety. I longed for us to take the

Enjoying the beauty of Switzerland, 1998

steamer across Lake Brienz then walk up to the Geisbach Falls and stand behind the thundering waterfall; to stroll up to the Barenplatz on a summers evening, listening to traditional Swiss music while watching the flag throwing; to take the cable car from Grindelwald to picnic in the alpine meadows, enjoying every day in the freedom that God had given me. And so we did.

We rely on a car to get around the counties surrounding our home town and had been praying for over a year for a replacement car, as the garage had told us that there were major problems looming which would, of course, bring major bills. As we neared the next MOT and all that that held, we continued to trust God for His provision. Though we could not see a way through we went on believing that He would not leave us stranded.

We decided to take a step of faith and, having seen a car that fitted our needs for sale in the local garage, we went for a test drive in it. It seemed perfect but, of course, the price was in the thousands and we could only stretch ourselves to a couple of hundred. As we drove by the garage a couple of weeks later, checking 'our car' was still there, I laughed and prayed, 'You can do anything, Lord, would you drop the price by a thousand pounds for us?' Imagine my amazement when that following Saturday I picked up the phone.

'Mrs Mancey, it's the garage. In case you're still interested in the car, you might like to know we've dropped the price by a thousand.' Our faith was mounting but our finances remained the same.

God gave a dream to someone who knew nothing about our need, telling them that we needed a car. They had a sum of money for some time that they had been asking God what they should do with, and so they came to us with a cheque. A few days later, another couple came to us with a cheque specifically, they said, for a car! We returned to the garage and, along with our own two hundred pounds, were able to buy the car with cash. His timing is perfect if we only persist in prayer and go on trusting Him.

The Lord teaches about giving, not just in terms of money but with time, possessions and indeed all the resources He has given to us. We need to learn to listen to His prompting to give and be instantly obedient. Not an easy lesson for many of us and one which God was eager to teach me. I prayed one of those dangerous prayers;

'Lord, teach me how to give more, show me whatever you want me to give and I'll give it.'

So He did. Within a few days of praying, a lady visited

work, stopped in my office doorway for a brief chat and, as she left, the Holy Spirit told me to give her my new bottle of Red Door perfume as a gift. I was shocked. This was an anniversary gift from Peter, only a couple of days earlier. Everyone knew me by my perfume and I loved it so much – surely this couldn't be God? What would I do if I gave it away? We couldn't afford to replace it.

I took it out of my handbag and sat and wondered if there was someway that I could pour half of it into a larger empty bottle I had at home. Suddenly, realising how I was thinking and being convicted by God of my meanness, I realised that I had to do this. After all, hadn't I just asked God to show me what to give and here I was the very first time wavering mightily in selfishness. There must be a reason He wanted me to do this. I rang Peter on his office phone.

'Hello lovely one. I have something to ask you. Would you mind if I gave my anniversary perfume away? I feel so awful asking.'

He laughed. 'Have you been praying again? Of course I don't mind. Go ahead.' I heard him chuckling as he replaced the receiver.

I typed a brief note and placed it and the perfume in an envelope and left it for this lady to find, disappearing rapidly home. The next morning as I walked into work she ran up and hugged me; my gift had really touched her life. There were things that only she and God knew about and this specific gift had spoken to her so much, bringing restoration and a fresh revelation of God's love and acceptance.

I had learned my first lesson in giving – just do it. However, God had not finished teaching me. That weekend, Peter and I took a Sunday morning service in a large parish an hour's drive from our home. We shared the speaking, both crammed into the pulpit together. We were speaking on faith and as a part of my testimony I felt prompted to share what God was teaching me about giving and trusting. I told them about my appalling wrestle over the perfume, which caused great laughter.

After the meeting a lady pressed a paper bag into my hand. As we got into the car the girls excitedly asked me to open it – presents were always appreciated. Inside was a huge bottle of Red Door along with smaller tubes of Red Door hand cream, shower gel and a handbag sized perfume! 'Give, and it will be given to you. Good measure, pressed down, shaken together, running over, will be put into your lap' (Luke 6:38).

On Monday morning, Peter opened the post only to find a gift of twenty five pounds – enough to replace my perfume, already posted by the time I had given my bottle away. Now we had been doubly blessed – how awesome is our Lord when we follow His prompting.

TEN

Trials and Triumphs

God used the teenage years of our girls to teach us much about faith, trusting Him for all circumstances and how to walk in His peace, no matter what is going on around us. My girls will tell you that this was one of my hardest lessons and I'm still learning! You may get a hint of my struggle to live a peaceful life during this time when I tell you that Victoria now refers to that period in our lives as 'the time when Mummy went mad!'

Watching your children maturing and becoming independent adults is one of the most difficult situations to live through. As a parent you want to protect them from all harm, save them from all their difficulties and disasters and be there to put everything right, even before it goes wrong! Of course, this is not possible but we tried and often failed. We found ourselves as parents in some very difficult situations as God began to challenge our level of trusting Him. We can all really believe we trust Him wholly but until anything is totally out of our control we never really know.

As the months went by our level of trust rose and with it our faith and confidence in our amazing God who showed us that He can truly accomplish the impossible and bring peace into every and all situations – if we will allow Him to. My admiration and love for our two wonderful girls has deepened so much over these past years. Their lives are truly in God's hands and we know He has the very best future and blessings stored up for them.

We learned much about the rightful fear of God. Not fearing Him as a father with a big stick waiting for us to get it wrong and punish us but fear of stepping outside of His will for our lives because we know He has the very best for us: that which would bring Him glory. God impressed upon us that it was time to return to the teaching centre in Lancaster where we had met so powerfully with Him over ten years before. We had a great sense that God wanted to further equip us and that He wanted to 'hone us up' once again. We enrolled on a year long training course. It is so easy in our busy lives, often full of good works, to become slack in our walk with God, to relax things at the edges, make compromises in our behaviour and attitudes, and squeeze God out of our time schedule. His only real desire is to spend time with us; He eagerly waits for us to come to Him.

As we walk as men and women of the Word and are open to His leading and prompting He will keep us sharp in our service for Him. Time with Him is our lifeblood and we realised that our spare time needed to be thought out once more. We were challenged by Him to fast and pray for future direction, not just fasting from food but from television, radio and reading other things for a forty day period. As it turned out, God began to speak to us in many ways and our forty days turned into a ten week period. Spending time with our Lord far outweighed anything else we had time for.

During this time we travelled up to Ellel Grange each month as we worked towards gaining their Modular Certificate in Healing and Discipleship. Part of the course involved training to lead a counselling session. We were grouped in threes, two of us as counsellors, the other as a counsellee, changing roles throughout the weekend. When the time came for me to be counselled, to my surprise I found God speaking into my life once more.

I had, I realised, through so many years of sickness and struggle evolved an understandable but nevertheless incorrect 'belief system' of my own. This had been compounded by others speaking words of discouragement about my health:

'Oh, you're always being ill, and your family, too.' This was, in fact, incorrect in many ways.

As someone with a disability, attention is often focused on what is wrong with you and seemingly that focus tends to extend to your family too. General sicknesses suffered by all – colds, coughs, infections – seemed to be homed in upon and became a regular battle for us against negative words, destined to drag us down. When you hear something over and over again, whether true or not, you begin to take it on board deep inside and it begins to bury God's truth. These beliefs about myself were so far down inside my thinking that even though I was a true Bible-believing, Spirit-filled Christian this belief system had blocked my ability to receive the Word of God in all its fullness.

I was astonished as God revealed this to me; a light went on in my mind, I was so excited. I knew that I had to renounce my wrong thinking, repent and ask the Lord for His forgiveness. As I did, I felt a huge weight lift off me. The enemy had been holding me into this lie throughout most of my lifetime. I found myself saying,

'I embrace the whole Word of God as my new and only belief system, front to back.' It felt as if I held the whole Bible in my arms, hugged into me.

As I returned home and began to walk out my new found, greatly increased freedom in Christ, the enemy, rather slow on the uptake, continued his attempts to squash me down, to whisper doubts and anxieties into my mind about myself and my family's future. It was incredible – like a shield around me these accusations fell away. All those declarations and promises I had spoken daily over myself and my family, though of course God had honoured them all, now took on new meaning and depth. There was such an increase of power behind them and I knew I was moving forward once again with a new revelation of God's Word at hand.

This embracing of the truth was soon put to the test as Becki, our eldest daughter, had embarked upon a nine month world trip. During her travels, she received a serious bite from a fire ant in Australia, which caused her ankle to swell badly. We began, in our prayers, to pray the Word over her and she recovered. Then came Singapore, just as the SARS[1] outbreak began. A close friend of her host family tragically died of the disease that same week. Rebecca's two week stay came to a close and she moved on to Seoul, South Korea. Within a short time she became ill.

This illness began whilst we were attending one of our training weekends. During the mid-afternoon teaching session, one of the team on reception slipped quietly into the room and touched my arm.

'Kate, your daughter is on the phone.'

I turned to Peter and took his hand and we quietly left the room and headed for the reception desk.

'Your daughter,' I thought, 'which one? It must be Victoria but why would she ring during the day?' As we approached the desk the receptionist held out the phone.

'Hello?' I held the phone to my ear and heard a distant rattling cough.

'Becki? Is that you?'

---

[1] Severe Acute Respiratory Syndrome

'Mummy, I feel awful, I'm so hot and this cough . . .' She stopped again as the cough overtook her.

'What's happened, lovely one?' I tentatively enquired. This was most unlike Becki, ringing from such a distance when she knew we were attending a teaching weekend. This could only be an emergency. Keeping my voice steady for her sake, though my heart was now racing, I again spoke into what sounded like a void.

'It's all right; tell me what's going on.'

'They think I have SARS. I've been to the doctor for tests and he gave me a paper bag full of different sized tablets. If I'm no better in two days I have to go back. I'm scared, Mummy.'

'It's all right, we'll pray, you're going to be fine.' As I spoke, I began to shake and Peter, standing behind me, put his arm around me realising that something was really wrong. We spoke for a few more minutes and then said goodbye, making arrangements to speak the following day.

I put down the receiver and turned to Peter, tears streaming down my face as I buried my head on his chest.

'It's Becki – they think she might have SARS.'

'Jesus, Jesus,' Peter whispered into my ear. 'Please go to our little girl right now and rescue her.'

We began to pray Psalm 91 over her life, reminding God of all His promises and refusing to allow doubts and anxieties to affect our minds: 'God says, "I will save those who love me and will protect those who acknowledge me as LORD. When they call to me, I will answer them; when they are in trouble, I will be with them. I will rescue them and honor them. I will reward them with long life; I will save them" ' (Psalm 91:14-16 GNB).

I needed a *rhema* word from God, a specific word for this situation. I sought Him day and night, and then, in the middle of the night as I lay on my pillow, tears pouring down my face, the Holy Spirit gave me direction.

He told me to breath over her in prayer seven times each day, praying that His breath would go through her lungs and keep her system fully cleansed and healed. I told no one of this at the time, as I was certain they would have thought I had really lost it this time! However, I knew deep inside that this was from God and despite all the desperate news reports, the doom and gloom merchants around us and, of course, the whispers of the enemy, God healed her and kept her in a place of safety throughout the remaining three months of her trip.

As we talked together on her return it transpired that her tremendous fever and hallucinations came to a climax during that particular night when I received God's *rhema* word. The fever broke as she prayed,

'Please Jesus, get Mummy to pray for me.'

It was at that very moment the Spirit gave me the instructions about breathing seven times. Walking through that time was exhausting but taught me much about perseverance in prayer and trusting in God's mighty saving power. I also discovered, sometime later, that the number seven was very significant, biblically, speaking of wholeness and perfection; our Lord is so amazing.

Our younger daughter Victoria was seeking work; in a rural area of England, not an easy task. Watching as she opened many letters of rejection to her job applications was so heart-breaking. She was so bored sitting around with nothing specific or terribly rewarding to do or anything positive to look forward to. The lack of income was more than difficult to handle too. She would smile at me whenever she was turned down from each job, as I would tell her once more that God must have something better for her. I believed it and, after a long wait, it came.

A college placement on a hairdressing course, coupled with an unexpected offer of work, which would lead to a full time position. How excited she was and how thankful we were that God had answered our prayers. This was indeed far better than she had hoped for and actually came as an unprompted offer, rather than through an application. Once again, God was showing us that He will find a way where there seems to be no way and that His love for each of us is so strong.

Our level of faith was to be severely tested soon after this blessing as, only a few weeks into her new college course, Victoria was knocked down by a car, suffering a head injury and deep concussion. We spent a desperate first week with her as she passed out many times, behaved like a small child and, most distressing of all, had lost most of her memory. At first she only knew Peter and me, and on seeing Becki commented on the length of her hair. This was a shock to us all as it had been almost a year before when Becki's hair had been short. Little by little with the great help of her sixth-form friends, who diligently came and regaled her with tales of events and friendships in college, the jigsaw pieces of memory were slowly put back into place. Even her then boyfriend had been forgotten, and we sat on the sofa together waiting to hear the roar of his motorbike as he came onto the driveway.

'What if I don't know him when he comes in?' she said, holding my hand. 'I'm really scared.'

For the first time as her mum I found myself unable to fully care for her, as she would sometimes pass out as she sat watching a film and dozing. My lack of sight was such a frustration to me as I had to keep waking her just to check she had only been asleep and not fallen into a deep faint, which necessitated reviving.

'Please help me Jesus,' I prayed. 'I want to look after her myself as I've always done.'

Again, we turned to our God, calling on the name of Jesus day and night, the Name above all names and all situations, to deliver and heal. As the weeks passed she regained her strength but her eyesight and memory were still affected. We prayed on, exhausted but knowing that somehow our compassionate Lord would restore her.

Within six weeks she was back at the hair studio three days a week and though there were a few frantic times when she passed out at work and had to come home, she battled on. However, she couldn't recall any of her college work or even the college itself and eventually decided to begin again the following September on a one year fast-track qualification. It was with such pride that we went, a year later, to see her receive her qualification. She had fought her way through the year, the final battle being a practical exam during the last few days of term, essential to her qualifying. She had tried over and over again to remember the procedure of plaiting and styling the hair but never made it within the time restriction. The last day came and we prayed as she left the house.

'Jesus, you gave her this course and her creative gift; she's worked so hard, please give her success today.'

We had a very excited Victoria on the phone later that day.

'I did it! I've passed! It was really strange, I can't explain it, as if time stood still and I just did it.' We smiled as we listened. Not strange at all, just our loving Jesus pouring out His blessing on His children.

Having successfully acquired a full time position in a local hair salon as a stylist, she continued to pass out on occasions making life extremely unpredictable and very worrying when waving goodbye every morning and won-dering if the phone would ring with another emergency. After a barrage of tests from the hospital, we visited the consultant to find out the outcome.

'Well, Victoria. You have signs of bruising on your brain but we can find no reason at all for you passing out so regularly.' We waited expectantly. 'It seems that you will just have to learn to live with it.'

'Live with it? How long for?' asked Victoria, a tremor in her voice.

'I'm afraid I can't say. It could be five years, it could be this Christmas.'

'Then we'll go for Christmas,' I interjected. 'Seems like the best option.'

I smiled. Faith had suddenly risen within me. I knew God was with us. The consultant discharged her and we left his room. I held Victoria's hand.

'Christmas it is then, only a few weeks to wait and Jesus is going to do it for you.'

She squeezed my hand and kissed me on the cheek: 'Thanks Mummy.'

Christmas came and went in the usual flurry of excitement, fun and laughter and great celebration. As we entered another new year I prayed each day.

'I believe you can do this, Jesus. She's your daughter, too, and your Word says that you are the healer. I'm trusting you.'

The weeks passed and my faith grew; months went by and by the summer I knew for certain that she was truly set free. Her last faint had been just before the year's end, and then freedom. 'So if the Son sets you free, you will be free indeed' (John 8:36).

Peter's mum, or Grandma-from-Essex, as she is affectionately known, came to stay with us over the previous Christmas holiday. We all sat one evening watching a favourite film, *Chariots of Fire*, which depicts the rivalry between two athletes, Harold Abrahams and Eric Liddle, and culminates in the 1924 Olympic Games held in Paris, France. It came to the part where the starting gun fired and the runners set off down the track, this time shown in slow motion. The crowds cheered their countries sprinters on

Family time together

and as I watched, my chair pulled up close to the television so I might see it more clearly, I saw, superimposed on the screen, crowds of angels in the stands chanting 'Peter and Kate, Peter and Kate'. There we were, racing down the track towards the finishing line, cheered on by the angels. I sat transfixed.

'What is this?' I wondered, 'What does it mean?'

Then, written before my eyes, came the date March 23rd. I sat back in the armchair and closed my eyes. 'What are you telling me, Jesus?'

I felt His presence, that familiar warmth holding me tight. What could this mean? What was going to happen on March 23rd? I didn't say anything that evening when the film had finished. As I lay in bed that night I silently prayed, 'I know you're with me always, so please show me when the time is right.'

The New Year came and went. From time to time I remembered that date, March 23rd. I worked out it was a Sunday.

'Perhaps God will speak to me again at church,' I thought.

How funny we are, as if that were the only time and place He can speak to us. I should have known by now that the Holy Spirit can communicate with us through anyone or anything at anytime and anywhere in ways that are so personal to us because He knows us better than we know ourselves.

Sunday, March 23rd arrived. God stayed silent.

'It can't have meant anything,' I mused that evening.

But I knew I'd seen that vision of the angels by the track side, cheering us as we began the race. I tucked it all to the back of my mind and once again prayed, 'If it was you, Lord, then show me what it means when I need to know.' Secure in the knowledge that He could and would do that, I fell into a deep and contented sleep.

Another year passed and by now we had left Torch and were stepping into our new work for the Lord. However, I had begun to feel very ill. I was always so tired and was losing weight rapidly. By the end of January, it was difficult to sit down for any length of time as my bones had no covering on them and every surface felt like concrete beneath me. I wore baggy clothes to conceal my skeletal figure, but one day in early February, suffering from an ear infection, I visited the GP. She was a lovely lady, who listened to me and then enquired, 'How are you doing in yourself these days? You're looking very pale. Have you lost weight?'

'I don't think so,' I lied. Fear began to grip me.

'I think we'd better have a look at you.'

'Oh no,' my mind cried out. 'Not again, please not again'. The old fear rushed into my mind . . . hospitals.

She was insistent and after a closer examination she

put her hand gently on my shoulder and said, 'I think I'm going to make you an appointment to see a gynaecologist as soon as possible. I'm sure it's nothing to worry about but we need to check this out.'

Trembling, I left her surgery and went straight into the arms of Peter.

'I have to go to the hospital to see someone. Something's horribly wrong with me, I know it is.' I held him tight. 'Oh Jesus,' I whispered. 'Please help me.'

The following week saw me in the local hospital. The examination over, I made my way to the ward sister to be booked in as soon as possible for an operation. She was kind but brisk.

'Let's get you weighed.'

I stood onto the scales. I now weighed under seven stone having lost a stone and a half. I was shocked now that reality had set in and I could no longer hide the truth.

'Let's see how soon we can fit you in,' she chattered on, turning the pages of her desk diary. 'February 17th?'

I paused, running through various dates in my mind.

'I'm sorry but I have a speaking engagement at the beginning of March and I need to know I'll be fit and well for that. It's been booked for a long time and I don't want to let them down.'

I was relieved to have an excuse – anything to put off the time of the operation.

'Hmm,' she frowned. 'The doctor wants you in as soon as possible.'

Her words filled me with more fear. 'Why the rush?' I thought. 'It can't be good.'

'You really must come in at the next available date, then.' She turned the pages of the diary once more. 'That will be Tuesday March 23rd.'

March 23rd. Immediately the presence of the Lord wrapped Himself around me. I saw the date once more before my eyes; the starting gun sounded and we began to run as the angels chanted our names, 'Peter and Kate, Peter and Kate.' Suddenly I knew it was going to be all right. I looked up at the sister.

'That's fine, March 23rd it is.'

How amazing that God should show me fifteen months earlier that on a certain date He was going to be with me and somehow that meant a new start, a new race and that the angels in heaven were cheering us on.

Now I had six weeks to wait and the fears began to hit me daily. But I knew God was with me and He would bring me through, He had shown me that. However, my old fear of hospitals rose up to taunt me. Memories of all I had been through came to mind throughout the day and night. In bed in the darkness I would sometimes shake with fear.

'Heal me, Lord, like you've done so many times before. I don't want to go through this again. What if I don't recover? What if it's too late?'

But God was about to show me that I could 'do things afraid' in order to conquer my fears and strengthen my faith and bring me to a greater place of peace. I tossed and turned and then reached for my Bible. Psalm 23 was to be my comfort and strength through those weeks. 'Even though I walk through the valley of the shadow of death, I will fear no evil, for you are with me . . .' (verse 4).

'You are with me, Jesus. You're going to take me through to the green pastures and quiet waters. I will trust you.'

I lay in the hospital bed on March 23rd, holding tightly to Peter's hand, waiting to go down to the operating theatre. I shook violently, gripped once again by fear but still reminding the Lord of His promises to bring me through. At last the time came to go.

'I love you.' Peter bent to kiss my cheek.

'I love you, too.'

As I entered through the theatre doors, I whispered,

'Jesus.' The peace of God enveloped me, my shaking ceased; relaxed and feeling so safe, I was lifted onto the operating table.

Lying in recovery on a trolley, I dazedly came round. Nearby, I heard the voice of the surgeon speaking to another lady.

'It went very well,' he said.

Then soft footsteps approached me. His hand patted mine. I struggled to speak.

'How did it go?'

He squeezed my hand gently. 'I'm sure it will be fine. I'll see you in six weeks with the results of the tests.'

With that, he walked away. My mind raced.

'I'm sure it will be all right . . .' Why did he say that to me and tell the other lady everything was fine? Already, fear for the future was pulling me down. Then I fell asleep only to wake back in bed again, with Peter sitting beside me.

'Hello sleepyhead. Like some water?' The iced water tasted wonderful as I sucked on the straw.

'Has anyone spoken to you about me?' I enquired nervously.

'No, not a word.' He gently stroked my cheek with the back of his hand. 'Don't worry, everything will be fine.'

'I'm trusting you, Jesus,' I thought, as once more I drifted back to sleep.

Six weeks later, having continuously battled with the fears and anxieties that tried to daily overwhelm my mind, I knocked gently on the consultant's door.

'Come in.'

I opened the door as he came towards me, offering me a chair to sit on. He returned to his desk, shuffled his notes and then looked across at me.

'Well, I won't keep you waiting any longer. Everything is fine, your results are clear and I won't need to see you again.'

The relief! My face lit up with a huge smile and my eyes sparkled once more.

'Thank you so much,' I grinned. 'That's great news.'

As he showed me out and Peter came to meet me, knowing by my face that all was well, I hugged him tightly.

'He did it,' I said. 'He brought me through and now we're in the race again.'

As we drove home full of joy we shared the contented peace of the day's happenings. We could move forward with confidence, a new confidence in the ability of God to go ahead of us and make the path straight.

We now had even greater faith and trust in the One who is able to bring us through any circumstance, strengthening and comforting us on the way. I can only say that walking with the Lord, led by His Spirit, is a truly exciting life with many challenges and testing times, mountain top and valley experiences.

As the writer to the Hebrews tells us, 'let us run with endurance the race that is set before us' (12:1). Learning to endure in different seasons has caused us to put down a firm foundation, strong roots as we find ourselves with all stripped away, fully dependent on God to bring us through the challenges that normal daily life brings. Serving God in our day to day work requires discipline and patience. Putting our confidence in God for His provision in many times of great need stretches our faith; so does battling in prayer through various new difficulties and learning to rest in all His Word promises.

In all these things we serve a faithful and mighty God. For all of us, in everyday life, there are often new challenges to be faced, unexpected happenings to contend with. An unexplained skin irritation and a different struggle with my digestion cause me to go through another trusting time with the Lord, for His strength in my weakness. Though fears for the future may bombard my mind from time to time as the enemy attempts to pull me down, now I know that as I whisper the name of Jesus, He will come to me as the comforter, deliverer and my 'strong tower' (Proverbs 18:10), where I can take refuge whilst the storm passes.

So, once again, I come before the One who heals and restores, the One for whom all things are possible, walking forward with Him into the future He holds for me, knowing that His desire is for us to be whole, for as the Word tells us, 'He took up our illnesses and carried our diseases' (Matthew 8:17) and 'By His wounds you have been healed' (1 Peter 2:24).

ELEVEN

A Hope and a Future

Housework is to most women never a delight and I'm no exception to that. However, there is something satisfying in having a clean, sweet-smelling home, piles of freshly washed and ironed clothing and a tempting meal cooking in the oven. Over the years, these daily tasks become second nature. I rarely now singe my finger with a hot iron, drown the ironing board whilst topping up the steam iron through that tiny hole, burn my arm whilst taking something out of the oven or turn a whole wash murky grey because of an overlooked coloured item.

I am only defeated by the pairing of the socks, a loathed job for the household and the only one in which I admit defeat. It is, therefore, a source of frustration when I encounter those who, with great emotion in their voices, hand placed on my arm, say,

'You must have a wonderful husband!'

'I have,' I reply.

It's true. Peter is a wonderful husband, we love each other very much, but they're not thinking of this as they move away, having given me a reassuring pat. They truly believe that he does everything for me – shopping, cleaning, cooking, baking, looking after the children, the bills, the organising of our day to day lives. Nothing I could ever

say would disprove this to them and so I don't attempt
it any more. The fact is, that just like any other woman,
almost all the running of the home, family and general
diary organisation is done by me, leaving Peter free to do
all that he has to do. We serve each other in this way, not
out of duty or need, but out of love.

Having now lived in our present home for fifteen years,
I can still clearly recall putting up the ironing board in the
dining room one afternoon only a few months after we had
moved in. I grimaced at the huge pile of washing on the
table waiting to be ironed and decided to listen to a Bible
teaching tape on cassette to help pass the time. Which tape
it was and what it was about I have no memory or record
of, but during that time God clearly spoke to me: 'Nine
years.'

This 'still small voice' hit me so powerfully that I
switched off my iron and sat down.

'Nine years,' I said to the Lord, 'What about nine
years?'

But that was all He said. I had a strong sense that
something would happen in nine years time and with my
human mind I began to work out how old we would all be
– much older as far as Peter and I were concerned and as
for the girls, Becki would be twenty two and Victoria eighteen; both adults, I mused. Then, coming to myself once
more, I stopped trying to out-think God! I placed this word
in God's hands and asked Him to bring it back to me if it
really was from Him. This is a prayer which we must all
learn to pray when we 'feel' God is speaking to us. I have
learned through the years that He will keep bringing it
before us if He needs us to remember but as long as we are
willing for His will to be done, He can also take it away.

Around seven years later we were driving to work early
one morning, again listening to a teaching tape, when God
challenged us. We had been introduced to many new Bible

teachers whose ministry had impacted our lives, including John and Lisa Bevere, Charles Stanley and Joyce Meyer, to name but a few, through the, then, Christian Channel (now GOD TV) founded by Rory and Wendy Alec.

I was so shocked at what He asked that I switched off the cassette player.

'Did I tell you that you would fulfil your calling at Torch?'

What did this mean? Surely we were called to Torch, to serve God there and we had assumed that this would be for ever. We had often sat in the Torch grounds during the summer months and mused on our future with a real sense of contentment. It was the word 'assumed' that God was jumping on. He had indeed called us to serve Him at Torch, but it seemed that He was now drawing our attention to the fact that maybe He had further plans for us. Our certain and steady road ahead, stretching to old age, was now littered with question marks.

That evening we sat before the Lord and asked Him to reveal His plans to us and of course, being like most people, expected revelation, a messenger angel or a prophet, at least, to knock on our door that very night. However, it was two years later after seeking God persistently, individually and together, with prayer and fasting, sometimes with tears and confusion, that He began to unfold His plan for us; this time truly as a couple working together, the desire of our hearts from the beginning. Throughout this waiting time God had much work to do in us in preparation for His next move. There are seasons in our lives when God needs to prune us: 'I am the true vine and my Father is the vinedresser. Every branch of mine that does not bear fruit he takes away, and every branch that does bear fruit he prunes, that it may bear more fruit' (John 15:1-2).

Pruning is often a painful process which, as more mature Christians, we need to submit to and even seek if we are to grow in the Lord. There are many behaviours and attitudes within us that are not honouring to God and certainly don't bring blessing to others. If we desire to be holy before the Lord then we need to be open to His teaching and discipline, just as a loving Father disciplines His children, still loving them with all His heart but desiring something greater for their lives. This pruning will equip us for the task ahead and only God knows what that is and what it will require of us. His refining fire is at work, testing us at every new level and giving us all the encouragement, strength and power we need to form character within us through His Holy Spirit.

We had learned so much about servanthood at Torch, being diligent in our work and honouring God in all we do, think and say. We are far from perfect in this but God knows our heart, our motives and desires. He continually pours out His grace upon us as we seek to give ourselves fully to the best of our ability.

During this time of seeking God for our future, we were unexpectedly invited to a leaders' conference run by our church's umbrella organisation, Newfrontiers. As we weren't in leadership at that time, this came as a great surprise but after prayer we knew God wanted us to go and this was confirmed by His financial provision. Prior to the four day conference we had to sign up for three seminars. An outline of each seminar was found on the conference website and so we sat in front of the computer one afternoon and Peter read through them. I was so depressed. Not only did I find it more than difficult to choose which ones I wanted to go to but I couldn't actually even understand what most of them were talking about! There was a list of about twenty and, to be honest, we chose through a process of elimination.

This random choice, or so we thought, was predestined by God. He continues to amaze me that even when we don't have a clue what we are doing, if we give it to Him, He can sort out everything. It was a truly remarkable four days; God led and instructed us session by session, building on what He had already spoken to us and confirming it all with His Word. He spoke to us about feeding His lambs and sheep together. He led us back to Isaiah 61, which had impacted our lives at the very beginning of our walk with Him. He gave us an even deeper love for those with broken hearts, in chains, living in dark places in their lives and those who needed to have their faith built up once more.

I cried so much as we drove home, as the Spirit of God touched us both whilst sharing all the amazing love and astonishing ability of our Lord to direct our paths: 'Trust in the Lord with all your heart and do not lean on your own understanding. In all your ways acknowledge Him and He will make straight your paths' (Proverbs 3:5-6).

One afternoon, some time later, whilst in the garden reading the Bible and just sitting thinking, a song came into my head from my Sunday school years;

Now Zacchaeus was a very little man
and a very little man was he,
he climbed up into the sycamore tree
for Jesus he wanted to see.

'Strange,' I thought, 'Why remember that?'

I sat and sang it through a few times and then God showed me a picture of a large tree, the sycamore, and He began to reveal that He wanted us to lift His people – those who felt crushed, bound and lost – up, as it were, into the tree, to a higher level, so that they could once again see Jesus and receive fresh faith and hope and all that He had for them.

I was so excited. As I sat there He seemed to underline

the word 'sycamore' and so, when Peter came home from work, we looked it up in the Bible dictionary. It told us that the sycamore was a tall tree with a V-shaped trunk and that the leaves were heart shaped. I knew God was showing me that we were to bring people up to a place, surrounded by His love, where they could once again see Jesus, just like Zacchaeus. Questions filled our minds and once more we found ourselves before the Lord giving Him all we had and submitting to Him totally, even praying that if we had got all this wrong that we were willing to stay where He had us forever. Over the next year we had a number of confirmations through His Word, prophetic 'words' and a sense of something about to happen.

One thing we knew, that God was calling us to further faith and trust in Him and His provision for us. This terrified us. It's one thing knowing it, even believing it, but doing it . . . ! We had experience of serving in a faith work and knew all about seeking God for His provision. We had recently been through a very hard time financially as it seemed that nearly all our household equipment broke down at the same time, the garden fence blew down in a storm and the car was written off during icy weather. Like a giant vacuum cleaner the little money that we had was sucked away. Now it seemed that God might be calling us to live without even an allowance.

I called out to Him, 'Can this really be right? You must show us if it is. It's too big a risk to take, too many responsibilities without hearing from you.'

The very next morning as we walked into church a lovely man of God, Charles, came straight up to us as we made our way to our seats.

'Kate,' he said, 'the Lord says that walking by faith is an exciting adventure in trusting in Him.'

I had to get him to repeat it to me; an answer so soon! God was truly with us.

We began to walk a very hard path, with our loyalties and love for our fellow workers at Torch coupled with the knowledge that just maybe God was re-routing us. We shared our thoughts with a very few godly friends in order that, once again, man's opinion would not get in the way of God's will and voice of direction. We had to, and indeed desired to, remain fully committed to where God had us and, like Moses, were not prepared to move at all unless God specifically showed us to: ' "If your presence will not go with me, do not bring us up from here" ' (Exodus 33:15).

The time came when we knew we had to take the step of faith, making the decision to leave Torch and offer ourselves again to the Lord as He increased the pressure on us to do so through His Word, teaching and prophetic words. We would begin by serving in our home church whilst continuing to pray for God's guidance for our future. We felt that He was now waiting for us to set a leaving date. Just as Peter stepped out of the boat onto the water (Matthew 14:22-33), not knowing what would happen but going in faith, God was telling us to step out and trust Him. Just like Abraham, we were to go first and then, having seen our trust in action, He would reveal His plans (Genesis 12:1). And so, after nine years of service at Torch, we made the decision to leave at Christmas. Having decided to go His peace filled our hearts, though we knew it would be hard to leave our lovely friends in the work of Torch. God was moving us forward once again.

Over the past six years, working as Mission Possible Ministries, God has opened doors in remarkable ways for us to minister His love and power through the teaching of His Word and the sharing of our testimony. We have received many invitations to lead church services, retreat days and Bible weeks, as well as being guest speakers at various meetings for church and other groups, including the *Alpha* course, Aglow International and the Full Gospel Businessmen's Fellowship International (FGBMFI). We have had the great privilege of seeing many lives transformed, restored and healed by His grace. Some have come to know our wonderful Jesus for the first time; others have recommitted their lives to Him and found fresh faith and purpose. Always, our loving Father in heaven receives them with such unconditional love and acceptance, no matter what their past has held.

Doris, an elderly lady in her late seventies, sat and wept with us one day during a retreat week. She told us of her life; as a little girl being taken from home to home with all she owned in a small bag. Often feeling abandoned she took the first opportunity she could to marry a man who could give her a home and the love she craved. However, once again she found herself in a harsh place, making do with second best in everything.

'The charity shop is good enough for you!' he had told her.

As she met with us, recently widowed after fifty five years of marriage, tears in her eyes, I held her hands in mine.

'I've never known what it is to be truly loved, cared for, wanted.' She squeezed my hands. 'I just want to be rid of this emptiness and hurt. I've never felt able to share this with anyone.'

We began to pray for her, that God would set her free from over seventy years of sadness. And He did. Her smile was reward enough as she hugged us.

'I feel so light and free. I'm going to begin a new life now,' she beamed.

When we met her four years later, dressed in her beautiful new clothes, the once timid and introverted old lady was full of fun and laughter and walking out her later years hand in hand with Jesus.

We were given the opportunity to return to the work of Torch through ministering at their Holiday and Retreat Centre in Sussex. We have spent many wonderful weeks each year leading worship and sharing God's Word and its application through personal testimony with many guests from both the UK and abroad. Throughout the weeks we have seen God touch hearts and watch lives unfold to become all He intended.

William arrived from Europe. He had lost his eyesight over twenty years before in an industrial accident. We met him on the first evening as the guests began to arrive, standing alone on the patio smoking a cigarette and unwilling to get into conversation with us.

'Oh Jesus, help us,' we prayed as we continued on our way to the bottom of the garden. We often stood by the garden gate, overlooking the South Downs, whilst asking God to help us. 'This man needs your love, help us to give it.'

On the second night we spoke about healing.

'Kate,' he interrupted. 'Since I began to know Jesus my life has got worse!' He was so angry.

The next evening we taught on forgiveness.

'Kate,' he interrupted again. 'There's a man in my church who has really hurt me and I just want to hit him!'

'Oh Jesus,' I silently prayed. 'This is terrible, what can we do?' I knew, of course. Just keep on loving him and God would do the rest. The next morning William came to see us.

'Peter and Kate, will you take these please?'

He held out packets of cigarettes and tobacco. With surprise, we did.

'You see,' he went on, 'as I lay in bed last night I thought about all you had said this week. Healing, forgiveness, God's love for me. I knew that I was only hurting myself and that I must forgive that man. So I did. Then God's

peace and joy filled me. I feel so different, so new, so full of life and I'm going home to make a new beginning, a new life and I don't want to smoke any more, either.' He smiled. 'With the money I save from giving up smoking, I've decided to come back next year.'

What a transformation! The remainder of the week was spent with much joy and laughter which spilled over into the whole group. What a remarkable God we serve. Truly, 'with God all things are possible' (Matthew 19:26).

And what of the future? It is safely in God's hands as we come to Him daily for further direction, trusting Him and putting our confidence fully in Him. He is certainly real and alive today through His Son, Jesus Christ, and through the power of the Holy Spirit we press on towards the goal, eternal life with Him (Philippians 3:14). But in the meanwhile we can experience and walk in His 'righteousness and peace and joy in the Holy Spirit' (Romans 14:17).

There is no other life worth living but the one He created us for. As we give our ordinary lives to Him He will lead us into all His extraordinary plans and purposes, meeting our every need through His grace, which He freely gives. And in turn, we may leave our own footprints of hope for those who follow behind.

Mission Possible Ministries

Bringing the healing power of God's love to His people

Since leaving the Torch Trust in 2003, Peter and Kate, under the Lord's leading, have worked as Mission Possible Ministries. Through this ministry they are seeing lives transformed through the teaching of God's Word and the sharing of personal testimony, bringing challenge, raising faith and renewing hope within the whole Body of Christ across all streams and denominations.

If you would like to contact Peter and Kate, please write to:

Mission Possible Ministries
PO Box 8526
Oakham
LE15 0BQ

E-mail: info@missionpossible.org.uk
Website: www.missionpossible.org.uk
Or go to: www.footprintsofhope.org